Eat
★ LIKE A ★
LUCHADOR

Interior and cover illustrations copyright © 2021 by Bene Rohlmann

Interior and cover photographs copyright © 2021; Pages 75, 227, 237 © George Tahinos; Pages 29 (bottom), 60, 63, 89, 90, 91, 107 (bottom), 113, 115, 139, 187, 194, 201, 212 (bottom) 220 (bottom), 301, 303 © Jerry Villagrana / JVDA Photography; Pages 139, 175, 177, 179, 199, 287 © Josh Garcia / Rudos Photography; Pages 11, 29, 51, 59, 95, 96, 105, 107 (bottom), 111, 119, 149, 157, 169, 185, 197, 201, 211, 223, 229, 241, 251, 259, 269, 289 © Oscar King Studios; Pages 19, 91, 142, 153, 207, 275, 290 © Jose "El Pollo" Gil; Pages 5, 23, 79, 125, 235 © Kevin Quiroz; Pages 65, 67, 99, 100, 215, 217 © Katie Grays; Pages 57, 143 © Daniela Herrerías; Pages 15, 123, 181, 233, 263 © Black Terry Jr.; Pages 107 (top), 161–164, 167, 212 (top) © Andres Aquino; Page 299 © Hayashi; Page 302 © Palehorse; Page 127 © Oli Sandler; Page 247 © Monkey Flip; Page 255 © Carxyus Fotograffía; Page 25 courtesy of Salina de la Renta; Page 35 courtesy of Sylvia Muñoz; Pages 41, 43 courtesy of Golden Era Lucha Tees

Running Press
Hachette Book Group
1290 Avenue of the Americas, New York, NY 10104
www.runningpress.com
@Running_Press

Printed in China

First Edition: June 2021

Published by Running Press, an imprint of Perseus Books, LLC, a subsidiary of Hachette Book Group, Inc. The Running Press name and logo is a trademark of the Hachette Book Group.

The Hachette Speakers Bureau provides a wide range of authors for speaking events. To find out more, go to www.hachettespeakersbureau.com or call (866) 376-6591.

The publisher is not responsible for websites (or their content) that are not owned by the publisher.

Print book cover and interior design by Celeste Joyce.

Library of Congress Control Number: 2020941896

ISBNs: 978-0-7624-9738-6 (hardcover), 978-0-7624-9739-3 (ebook)

1010

10 9 8 7 6 5 4 3 2 1

BARRIGA LLENA, CORAZÓN CONTENTO.
Full stomach, happy heart

This book is first dedicated to the families of lucha libre. It has been an honor and privilege to not only grow up as a proud Mexican, with our amazing and wonderful traditions, but to also be part of the world of lucha libre—both my own extended family and the entire extended familia de la lucha libre.

★

CADA MAESTRILLO TIENE SU LIBRILLO.
Each person has their own way of doing things

I also dedicate this book to the fans of our amazing sport without whom the world of lucha libre would not continue to exist. So now, I want to share with you a look inside both our rich traditions and many "family secrets."

★

"TODAY IS ESPECIALLY DELICIOUS."
Nacho (Jack Black) in Nacho Libre

And to those who know nothing of either lucha libre or Mexican culture, except for what they may see on a screen, I welcome you to join us on this journey and learn about both worlds as one.

Eat LIKE A ★ LUCHADOR ★

THE OFFICIAL COOKBOOK

LEGENDS OF LUCHA LIBRE & MÓNICA OCHOA

RUNNING PRESS
PHILADELPHIA

TABLE OF
CONTENTS

INTRODUCTION

I N 2018, THE government of Mexico declared *lucha libre* to be "an integral part of the culture of Mexico." In the more than eighty years since the sport had been formally introduced to our country by Salvador Lutteroth, tens of millions of Mexicans had become die-hard aficionados, and millions upon millions more around the world had fallen in love with the colorful and acrobatic form of entertainment. For some, the love began the first time they attended a live match. For others, it was when they first saw awe-inspiring *luchadores* doing battle on their TV screen. And in some cases, like mine, you are literally born into it.

But, the story really begins long before I was born...

In the 1950s, my great-grandfather, Rafael Barradas Osorio, held the position of secretary in the Boxing and Wrestling Commission of Mexico City. Over his thirty-eight years in this role, he would make many decisions that would forever change the course of lucha libre. In fact, my great-grandfather became known as the "Iron Commissioner" because of his strict way of running the business.

It is fairly well known that machismo was, and will continue to be, a part of the lucha libre and combat sports worlds. Any business in which one's physical looks and abilities are on display tends to lead to puffed-up chests and an overly competitive nature. Such a business also tends to be one that is not very kind to outsiders or changes, especially when that world has secrets to it that help protect the lines of where fight and performance begin and end. My great-grandfather exemplified these aspects, upholding machismo and protecting secrets of the trade. Mexico is also very strongly tied to men and women having traditional roles within a family and community. And, to my great-grandfather, a woman's place was absolutely not in a lucha libre ring. In fact, because of his decree as the Iron Commissioner, women's wrestling was banned in the capital of Mexico for thirty-three years.

Perhaps it was some sort of cosmic karma, but just imagine that you are a man respected by everyone around you. Now imagine that your principles and ideology are called into question, not just by anyone, but by your very own granddaughter!

At the age of fourteen, Bibiana Ochoa Barradas was already a rebel—not as a luchadora, but as a musician who imagined life beyond her hometown of Zamora, Michoacán, and dreamed of the big capital city of Mexico. The young woman, who would later in life become known as Estrellita, played keyboard in a band called Los Rudos del Ritmo. And it just so happened that the other members of the group were luchadores, some of them among the most famous, such as Ari Romero, Kung Fu, the Panther, Mario Prado, Buffalo Wild, and Gran Apache. As fate would have it, Bibiana would begin training to become a luchadora under a fighter by the name of El Hijo del Gladiator. It was around this time that she also met a luchador then known as Jerrito Estrada, with whom she would fall in love and have two children.

Being a luchadora is never an easy path. Being a rebel against your own grandfather is an even harder path to take. But, in 1993, two years after her luchadora debut, Estrellita became pregnant with her first child, and two years after that, she gave birth to me!

Unfortunately, shortly after, my parents' relationship ended. My mother, who was still very young, only twenty years old at the time, had to take care of her two children by herself, which motivated her to become a star. In her eyes, if she could become a top luchadora, she could provide for her family very well and do it all on her own terms. It would also prove to her parents and grandparents that she had not wasted her career chasing a silly dream that was the antithesis of what they expected of a Mexican mother. In 1997, she joined the most popular lucha libre promotion on Mexican TV—Lucha Libre AAA.

It may sound extraordinary to be the child of luchadores, but in reality it is very complicated. Lucha libre is an all-absorbing job that forces you to miss significant moments in the lives of your loved ones, like their first words, their first missing tooth, their first steps, school festivals, and school achievements, including graduations. In my case, having a single mom, I always had the care and attention of my grandmother. While my mother was touring with AAA, my *tita* (aunt) took the place of my mom.

When my mom had a lucha libre show near where we lived, she would take me with her, and that's when my own love for lucha libre was born. Part enamored with the show of it all, part wanting to follow in my mother's footsteps, I knew that

I wanted to do something in the business. But my mom's advice was to focus only on my studies and to enjoy sports as an amateur. I decided to study communication and then apply my skills toward a career in the industry that I loved. Much as my mother found herself fighting to break into a male-dominated field in the ring, I, too, have had to follow her luchadora spirit to make my way in the heavily male-dominated and guarded world of lucha libre journalism.

Aside from photography, where the ratio is a bit more even, nearly all other positions related to covering or analyzing lucha libre are absolutely dominated by males. The number of female lucha reporters and interviewers in Mexico today can still be counted on one hand. I find myself very lucky to be among them and to have my work featured on LuchaCentral.com, the first (and only, as of this writing) bilingual lucha libre and professional wrestling news site—the site many consider the ESPN.com of lucha libre.

Having grown up in a lucha family, one of my most favorite subjects to cover is that of the importance of family within the sport. While it is not uncommon for a child to follow in their parent's footsteps in any career (many current WWE wrestlers in the United States are second- or third-generation wrestlers), in lucha libre, family and tradition are on a whole different level. Some families have ten or more members who have all become luchadores and luchadoras.

With this cookbook, I wanted to share the family traditions and favorite dishes of the stars of our incredible sport with recipe seekers and lucha libre fans and enthusiasts around the world. I wanted to collect the rich and varied stories of Mexico's iconic sports entertainers—from multiple-branched lucha dynasty family trees and the luchadores who broke out of Mexico and became global stars in the 1990s to today's hottest up-and-coming stars, to individuals who simply worked hard and persevered to make it on their own, like my mother.

As I started thinking about how I wanted to share the colorful and family-filled world of lucha libre with others, it felt natural to incorporate one of the other biggest parts of family and culture in Mexico—our food. And thus, the idea for this cookbook was born.

As with so many other cultures, food is an essential part of Mexico and Mexican tradition. It truly brings families together and recipes are often passed on from generation to generation. And although you may recognize a particular dish by name in the pages that follow, you may not be familiar with the manner in which the particular region or family from which the luchador comes has influenced the version of their recipe that appears in this book.

I also wanted to reach beyond only those who spend their career inside the ring and include some of the most important aspects of lucha libre outside the ropes. The family of the first female promoter of lucha events in Tijuana shares one of her classics. Former WWE World Champion Rey Mysterio's personal mask maker may live in Japan, but he fondly remembers drinking *tepache* when in Mexico and shares with me how he now makes it while living more than 7,000 miles (11,265 km) away. From photographers to company owners, the more than sixty-five contributors to this book all share a love for both lucha libre and the cuisine of Mexico.

Within these pages, I have of course included some traditional Mexican must-haves, such as *albondigas*, huevos rancheros, *caldo de res*, and *enfrijoladas*, but you will also find traditions that today's luchadores are passing down to their own families, such as Rey Fenix's MexaKing Wrap and Solar's version of Aztec cake (which is not a dessert at all and more of a lasagna).

Because it has not only been Mexicans who have embraced the lucha libre style and spirit, I also talked with a number of wrestling stars who either began their career in lucha libre, such as WWE Hall of Famer Amy Dumas (aka Lita) and Filipino American superstar TJ Perkins, or those who traveled to Mexico to study the style later in their career, such as Canada's Taya Valkyrie and Japan's Kikutaro.

I also wanted to be sure to include in the book some modern twists on classic recipes, such as chicken chorizo chimichangas and a vegetarian version of a classic chicken chile verde.

From appetizers to main dishes and from delectable desserts to Mexico-mixology-inspired drinks, I am proud to share these family and fighter traditions and to show you how to eat (and drink) like a luchador!

MÓNICA OCHOA
MEXICO CITY, MEXICO
2021

featuring

APPETIZERS

★ CAIDA UNO ★

MUELAS DE GALLO

 TORREÓN, COAHUILA, MEXICO

MUELAS DE GALLO is a Mexican rapper and member of La Banda Bastön, a group known for its love of lucha libre.

Muelas remembers first seeing lucha libre on television as a child. He would watch EMLL (now CMLL) and fell completely in love with the sport, thanks to the characters, masks, and stories. Like so many fans, while growing up, he and his brother would play and wrestle with each other, imitating their favorites, but it was not until his teenage years that he was actually able to attend a live lucha libre event. As his love for wrestling grew, he started following American and Japanese companies as well and came to be very knowledgeable about the industry in general.

This love and dedication to lucha libre resulted in the launch of *Los Reyes del Biutiful* on Spotify in 2016, the first major independent Spanish-language lucha podcast. Hosted by Muelas along with fellow urban music maker Cat Scratcho (DJ of Lng/SHT), the show finds them interviewing different luchadores and wrestling personalities.

Past guests have included new second-generation lucha star and WWE superstar El Hijo del Fantasma, third-generation luchador Tiger Casas (see his recipe on page 297), and the legendary, groundbreaking, former WWE World Champion Rey Mysterio.

Muelas was born in Torreón, Coahuila, but moved to Mexicali, Mexico, at a young age, and considered Baja California his home. The northernmost state in Mexico, sharing a border with the US, Baja is known for its warm climate, beaches, and surf-inspired cuisine. Whereas on the US side of the border, you may find a Starbucks on every corner; in Baja, you're quite likely to find a restaurant, shop, or cart selling a local favorite—ceviche. With Baja surrounded on three sides by water, fresh fish and seafood are never far. Putting his unique spin on a recipe that encompasses the flavors and vibe of Muelas's city well, this recipe represents his not-so-common take on a traditional dish commonly prepared for family gatherings, afternoons with friends, birthdays, or any day of the week.

CEVICHE (TUNA COCKTAIL)

SERVES
4 to 6

1 raw serrano chile

10 dried chiltepín chile pods
(optional)

1 garlic clove

Juice of 1½ lemons

Sea salt and freshly ground black
pepper

1½ pounds (680 g) tuna steak, cut
into ½-inch (1.3 cm) cubes

½ medium-size red or white onion,
chopped

1 medium-size cucumber, heart
and seeds removed, cut into
½-inch (1.3 cm) cubes

1 Paradise or Haden mango,
peeled and pitted, cut into
½-inch (1.3 cm) cubes

4 teaspoons (20 ml) tomato-clam
juice (e.g., Clamato)

Serving Suggestion

Serve on toast smeared with
mayonnaise.

In the temperate climes of seaside Mexicali, simple dishes that don't require a hot oven reign supreme. This tuna cocktail dish is uncomplicated in its preparation but delivers plenty of fresh flavor that evokes a sunny day at the beach.

Although Muelas de Gallo originally picked up this recipe from his brother, he has spent years developing it and refining it to his own unique taste. It makes for an elegant appetizer at family gatherings and special events, but it's also easy enough to whip up on a lazy afternoon or any time you're craving a taste of the sea.

1. In a molcajete (mortar and pestle) or in a food processor, grind the serrano chile until completely crushed. Add the chiltepín pods and crush, mixing them with the serrano chile. Repeat the same process with the garlic. If using a food processor, transfer the mixture to a large bowl before proceeding.
2. Add about three-quarters of the lemon juice; add sea salt and black pepper to taste. Mix with a spoon.
3. Add the chopped tuna. Stir to combine.
4. Add the chopped onion. Stir to combine, then add the remaining lemon juice.
5. Add the cucumber and mango. Stir to combine.
6. Add the tomato-clam juice and mix one last time to incorporate. Season with additional salt and pepper to taste.

9

AMAZONA

 TIJUANA, BAJA CALIFORNIA, MEXICO ◆ NOVEMBER 2011

AS A YOUNG girl, Amazona would watch lucha libre with her grandfather, who was a big fan. She loved to shout at the vile *rudos* and would get excited when the *técnicos* won their matches. She would show her support of her favorites by getting photos and autographs from them.

When she was twelve years old, Amazona accompanied her brother, who was training at the world-famous Rey Misterio gymnasium in Tijuana, to class one day. The gym is famous for producing many top luchadores, including Konnan, Rey Mysterio, Psicosis, Damian 666, Halloween, and Misterioso, and even had a hand in training Eiji Ezaki (aka Hayabusa).

She enjoyed the training and continued to go while her brother was there, to pass the time. When, years later, it was time for her brother to take his test to become a licensed luchador, her trainers also convinced her to take the test as well. Not expecting to pass, she did well enough to gain her license as a professional luchadora.

After she passed the test, she discussed with Rey Misterio Sr. what her name should be and he suggested "Amazona." Knowing Rey Misterio Sr.'s wife used the same name when she competed, Amazona took this as a huge compliment.

As a luchadora, Amazona wrestled throughout Baja California and across the border in Southern California, her home arena being the famous Auditorio de Tijuana. Her husband, also a luchador, wrestles under the name Venum Black. Husband and wife have captured numerous championships in lucha libre and the name Amazona is the perfect way to describe her style as a luchadora.

CHEESE BALL

MAKES ABOUT
24
appetizer-size servings

1 pound (455 g) cream cheese, at
    room temperature

2 tablespoons (28 g) mayonnaise

2 tablespoons (12 g) finely chopped
    green onion

2 tablespoons (19 g) seeded and
    finely chopped red bell pepper

1 teaspoon (5 ml) Worcestershire
    sauce

1 teaspoon (5 ml) freshly squeezed
    lemon juice

½ cup (110 g) chopped nuts, pecans
    recommended

Serving Suggestion

To serve, place the cheese ball on
a plate surrounded by an array of
items to dip: crackers, tortilla chips,
toasts, celery or carrot sticks, slices
of bread, etc.

What's not to love about cheese balls? They're a little
kitschy, plenty festive, and totally tasty.

This recipe comes from Tijuana-based luchadora
Amazona, and, rest assured, it's anything but boring.
Worcestershire sauce, green onion, and red bell pepper
add a little bit of feisty flavor to this nut-covered orb of
dairy delight.

But is it a meal or just a starter? For a luchador, a bit of
both. According to Amazona, "For me, it's food, but it can
also be a snack."

1. In a large bowl, mix together the cream cheese and mayonnaise until fully incorporated and creamy.

2. Add the rest of the ingredients, except the chopped nuts.
Mix well.

3. Put the entire bowl in the refrigerator for about 1 hour.

4. Near the end of the chilling period, scatter the chopped nuts
in a large, shallow bowl.

5. Remove the mixture from the refrigerator; form into a ball
with your hands. Roll the ball in the nuts until it's completely
coated.

6. Wrap the nut-covered cheese ball with plastic wrap, taking
care not to lose the round shape. Put the ball back in the
refrigerator and let chill for several hours, or until firm.

See page 68 for Amazona's Caldo de Pollo recipe.

SAM ADONIS

 MONROEVILLE, PA • **FEBRUARY 2008**

NOT MANY KIDS grow up and get to say "I told you so" in regard to their childhood dream; however, Pennsylvania native Sam Adonis is the exception. Since he was a young child and born into a wrestling family, Sam's dream was always to become a pro wrestler. In 2008 that dream came true when he made his pro wrestling debut.

Adonis was trained at a young age by his older brother—pro wrestler and current WWE color commentator Corey Graves. As a result of hard work and guidance, Sam would go on to sign with WWE in 2011 but unfortunately was injured after just two matches with WWE's then developmental promotion Florida Championship Wrestling (FCW). From there, Sam would find success traveling the globe.

He became the first American ever to win the British Heavyweight Championship in England and go on to defend the championship in Mexico's Desastre Total Ultraviolento (DTU) promotion on May 1, 2016, marking his first match in the country.

A few weeks after his Mexico arrival, Adonis began working for the oldest and one of the most respected wrestling companies in the world,

Consejo Mundial de Lucha Libre (CMLL). He immediately entered into the main event slot and would pitch a Donald Trump–supporter gimmick that would garnish more heat than any luchador had seen in Mexico in twenty years.

Adonis competed in the International Grand Prix in 2016 and would go on to headline and sell out Arena México on August 4, 2017, in a Hair vs. Hair match, which he won, against the legendary Blue Panther. A few months later on New Year's Day, another legendary luchador, Negro Casas, would challenge Adonis for his locks and succeeded in pinning the then-twenty-seven-year-old, thus shaving his head. From there, Sam began working with legendary Japanese wrestler Último Dragón, feuding across three different countries. The path would eventually take Adonis to work multiple tours with All Japan Pro Wrestling (AJPW).

Sam's most recent endeavor has involved the creation of his own Pittsburgh-based promotion WrestleRex, where Adonis is currently viewed as a hometown hero, all while maintaining the "Hottest Heel" global moniker and continuing to live that childhood dream.

DIABLA SHRIMP

SERVES
4

SAUCE:

3 guajillo chiles, seeded

3 chiles de arbol

1 garlic clove, finely chopped

¼ medium-size white onion, finely
   chopped

1 chipotle chile, finely chopped

Salt and freshly ground black
   pepper

SHRIMP:

2 tablespoons (28 g) unsalted
   butter

1 garlic clove, minced

1 teaspoon (3.3 g) finely chopped
   onion

4 cups (1½ pounds [680 g])
   medium fresh shrimp, peeled,
   deveined, tail off

Kosher salt

TO SERVE:

4 large romaine lettuce leaves,
   washed

4 crackers

When Sam Adonis hit Arena México in 2016, he may have had more heat with the crowd than the devil himself, so he was right at home with any dish with the name *diabla* or *diablo* in it.

There was a little place near the arena that had the best shrimp Sam had ever eaten in Mexico—now that he's back traveling the globe, he's always looking for a way to eat a good shrimp dish. This is an easy version to prepare at home, featuring shrimp in a diabolically delicious spicy sauce. With three different types of chile peppers, it's perfect for heat seekers.

1. Make the sauce: Combine ½ cup (120 ml) of water with the guajillo and de arbol chiles, garlic, and onion in a medium-size saucepan. Cook over medium heat for about 30 minutes.

2. Remove from the heat and transfer to a blender. Add the chipotle chile and blend until smooth. Transfer the sauce back to the saucepan; add salt and pepper to taste. Keep the mixture warm by covering with aluminum foil.

3. Cook the shrimp: Melt the butter in a skillet over medium heat. Add the garlic and onion; once the onion is softened and lightly browned (about 3 minutes), add the shrimp and a pinch of salt and sauté for 3 to 5 minutes, until pink and appearing fully cooked.

4. Once cooked, transfer the shrimp to the saucepan containing the prepared sauce and coat the shrimp with the sauce.

5. Divide the shrimp and sauce among the lettuce leaves and serve with crackers on the side.

MORE

HEAT
THAN
the
devil himself!

PREP MINCE ONIONS.

TAYA VALKYRIE

FROM **VICTORIA, CANADA** • DEBUT **DECEMBER 2010**

TAYA VALKYRIE'S ENTRANCE into lucha libre comes from a very unlikely path. At a young age, Taya showed her love for athletics and competition. When she was four years old, she started with gymnastics, which was followed by dance, including ballet. Her experience with those eventually led to fitness competitions and modeling, where she went on to be featured in magazines and win awards. Following the path of a number of successful female WWE Superstars of the '90s before her, Taya decided to parlay her fitness modeling career into a shot at the world of pro wrestling. It was the later lucha twist that no one, not even Taya, saw coming.

Growing up in Victoria, British Columbia, Taya traveled to Calgary to train in wrestling with veteran wrestler Lance Storm. After completing training at Storm Wrestling Academy, she was signed to a WWE developmental contract. In the days before Florida's WWE Performance Center existed as a hub for developmental talent, Taya

remained wrestling in Canada and eventually decided to take the ultimate gamble on herself.

Speaking no Spanish at all and never having been to that country, Taya took a booking in Mexico for the Perros del Mal promotion and was planning to stay for six months. She was so impressive that the company's owner and headlining star, Hijo del Perro Aguayo, asked her to stay even longer, becoming a member of the Perros del Mal group—the most popular faction in all of lucha libre. As a member of Perros del Mal, she began working for Lucha Libre AAA, one of the largest pro wrestling companies in the entire world.

Taya decided to immerse herself in the culture and learned to speak Spanish, which helped her gain a following in Mexico. Working for AAA, she managed to capture the AAA Reina de Reinas championship three times and won the title of Luchadora of the Year in back-to-back years. Her first reign lasted a record shattering 945 days, an incredibly long run for any champion in modern

pro wrestling, let alone a relatively new foreigner. "La Wera Loca"—as she became known in Mexico—went from a complete newcomer to the most popular female *gringa* (non-Mexican) in the then twenty-year history of AAA in an unfathomably short time.

While working for AAA, she debuted alongside Johnny Mundo on the TV series *Lucha Underground*, a groundbreaking concept from both the Mexican lucha company and director Robert Rodriguez. Taya was able to work on all four seasons of *Lucha Underground*, which helped give her exposure to fans in the US and around the world. The irony that it took becoming a star first in Mexico to become known throughout the US and her home country of Canada was not lost on her.

In 2017, Taya debuted for IMPACT Wrestling, where she would perform weekly as opposed to *Lucha Underground*'s more traditional "seasonal"

approach to TV. On January 6, 2019, she defeated Tessa Blanchard to win the IMPACT Knockouts Championship and would go on to hold the title for more than one year, becoming the longest-reigning champion to hold that title.

Outside the ring, Taya has produced a short horror film called *The Iron Sheik Massacre* alongside her husband, WWE superstar John Hennigan (aka John Morrison), and she is the proud pet-mother of social media–popular pooches Presley and Bowie, who can be followed at @The_Prince_P and @Bows_Malone, respectively, on Twitter and collectively @the_pee_boyz on Instagram. In fact, Presley is so famous that he is even being turned into a sidekick for the release of a Taya Valkyrie action doll in a line called I Am Brilliance, which celebrates careers for women—and what a career Taya has had so far! And, if you ask her, the best is yet to come.

LOCA GUACAMOLE

SERVES
6 to 8

2 jalapeño peppers, stems removed

2 to 4 garlic cloves, crushed, or to taste

Juice of 2 limes

Kosher salt and freshly ground black pepper

4 ripe avocados, peeled and pitted

1 medium-size tomato, chopped into ½-inch (1.3 cm) pieces

Holy guacamole! Sorry, couldn't resist. For guacamole lovers who like it hot, this recipe from Taya Valkyrie is gonna be just right.

A few things separate this recipe from traditional guacamole. For one, it packs plenty of heat. A hefty serving of jalapeños will bring a tear to your eye—in a good way. Second, the guacamole is pulsed in a food processor to reach a creamy, smooth consistency, but you have the freedom to add more texture depending on how coarsely you chop the tomatoes that are folded in directly before serving.

This recipe is the perfect accompaniment to *carne asada*—check out Valkyrie's Carne Asada Marinade recipe on page 78.

1. In a food processor, mince the jalapeños; if you're not a fan of spice, remove the seeds first.
2. Once chopped, add the crushed garlic, lime juice, and salt and black pepper to taste. Pulse for 30 seconds.
3. Add the avocado and pulse for about 30 seconds, or until it has achieved your desired consistency.
4. Transfer to a serving bowl; fold in the chopped tomato directly before serving.

SALINA DE LA RENTA

 CAROLINA, PUERTO RICO • **SEPTEMBER 2016**

SOMETIMES THINGS WORK out even when they don't go according to plan. Case in point: the career of Salina de la Renta.

The Puerto Rican was trained as a wrestler and wrestled for three years as both Salina and as Mila Naniki before being sidelined with an injury. It turned out to be a blessing, as the injury allowed Salina to transition into managing when she joined Major League Wrestling in 2018.

As the leader of the Promociones Dorado stable, Salina has managed such top luchadores as the Lucha Brothers and LA Park, and even non-luchadores, such as Low Ki, all while establishing herself as one of the top on-camera wrestling industry talents in the world—and while still only in her early twenties. There's no telling what the limit is for a woman who walks the walk and most definitely talks the talk.

FUN FACTS

★ Salina de la Renta also does announcing for MLW's Spanish Commentary, the first female Spanish pro wrestling commentator in US TV history. She became the first Latina to executive produce a televised episode of professional wrestling after producing a taping of MLW Fusion in 2019.

★ She's part of the management team of lucha libre–inspired clothing line RUDA (taking its name from what a "bad girl" is called in lucha libre).

★ She won the American Combat Wrestling Championship in 2017, holding it for 287 days before vacating the title due to injury.

PUERTO RICAN CORNBREAD

MAKES
9
servings

Cooking spray, for pan

1 cup (140 g) cornmeal

1 cup (125 g) all-purpose flour

1 cup (200 g) sugar

1 tablespoon (scant 14 g) baking powder

1 teaspoon (2.3 g) ground cinnamon

¼ teaspoon (1.6 g) kosher salt

1 (12-ounce [354 ml]) can evaporated milk

8 tablespoons (1 stick, 113 g) unsalted butter, melted and slightly cooled

2 large eggs, lightly beaten

1 teaspoon (5 ml) pure vanilla extract

Serving Suggestion

Feel free to cut these into fewer servings for hungry warriors. Salina claims that it's so good she can polish off a whole pan herself.

Luchadoras are hard to fit into a box. Sure, they're warriors, but they're also extremely loving and nostalgic, especially when it comes to their family. Salina de la Renta defies simple classifications, too. First, she went from luchadora to manager and then became the first Hispanic woman to executive produce an episode of pro wrestling TV, and she continues to blaze new multihyphenated trails.

This recipe for cornbread comes from Salina de la Renta's great-grandmother, and it similarly defies categorization. Is it a breakfast bread? A side dish? Dessert? The answer to all three is *yes*. It's all about how you serve it and how you top it.

This recipe yields an assertively, but not aggressively, sweet cornbread and you can personalize it to suit your needs. Want it as a savory side? Throw some jalapeños into the batter. Craving a breakfast bread? Top it with butter and honey. Looking to go decadent? Toast a slice and serve it with ice cream.

1. Position a rack in the middle position in the oven. Preheat the oven to 350°F (180°C). Generously spray an 8-inch (20.5 cm) square baking pan with cooking spray.

2. In a large bowl, sift together the cornmeal, flour, sugar, baking powder, cinnamon, and salt.

3. In a separate bowl, mix together the evaporated milk, butter, eggs, and vanilla.

4. Stir the dry ingredients into the wet, mixing only until everything is moistened. Spoon the batter into the prepared baking pan.

5. Bake for 30 minutes, or until lightly browned on top and a toothpick or knife inserted into the center comes out mostly clean. Remove from the oven and transfer to a wire rack to cool.

"KING FATBOY" PAPO ESCO

 THE BODEGA (SAN JOSE, CA) • FEBRUARY 2016

IN A WORLD where professional wrestlers are viewed as powerhouse musclemen, high-flying daredevils, or technical wizards, one thing is true: Wrestlers around the world are working hard to be a type. That is, except one. Papo Esco isn't any of those types. As a matter of fact, because he doesn't fit into the stereotypical mold of a professional wrestler, he's created his own mold—the mold of the King FatBoy.

Wearing this mantra across his belly every time he sets foot in the ring, Papo's mission is clear—leave a mark on an industry that doesn't look at him as anything more than something he's embraced strongly—a FatBoy. Prove that all the muscles, high flying, and technical wizardry don't mean a thing when you're looking up at the lights, gasping for air, 'cause you've been mauled by a gorilla. Show them all that someone they didn't choose as the "one" is better than everybody—in the ring, on the microphone, and in front of the camera.

Papo intends to reignite the spark that is Bam Bigelow, One Man Gang, King Kong Bundy, and every FatBoy that came before him. He's ready to strike a match and set the wrestling world on fire, his way. Papo goes by many names: the Lucha Thug, the One Man Lucha Gang, Rey Gordo. But his life work will be defined as a king. All hail the King FatBoy, Papo Esco.

FUN FACTS
(Papo hates fun.)

* Papo trained at Pro Wrestling Revolution Training Academy under the tutelage of Gabriel Ramirez, Skayde, Lady Apache, Vinnie Massaro, and Robert Thompson.
* The beatdowns this bully has given in the Bay Area of California have garnered him both the Pro Wrestling Revolution and All Pro Wrestling Tag Team Championships, while notable opponents have included Texano Jr., Psycho Clown, Skayde, Chavo Guerrero Jr., and MVP.
* Has also appeared on World Wrestling Entertainment and New Japan Pro-Wrestling broadcasts.

RELLENOS DE PAPAS

MAKES
12 to 18
rellenos

2 to 3 pounds (905 g to 1.4 kg)
medium-size russet potatoes,
peeled and cut into quarters

Salt and freshly ground black
pepper

1 large egg, lightly beaten

¼ cup (32 g) cornstarch, plus more
for dusting hands

2 pounds (905 g) ground beef

2 pounds (905 g) shredded
Cheddar cheese

Serving Suggestion

Papo loves serving this recipe with
his own special sauce. Combine 1
part ketchup, 3 parts mayonnaise,
and a dash of sofrito, garlic, hot
sauce, or adobo (your choice). Mix
together, chill for a few minutes,
and dip away!

Luchador Papo Esco, known as the Bully from the Bodega,
was raised by a single mother who had to work very hard to
keep her children fed and cared for. When it came to meal-
times, it was important to create dishes that were inexpen-
sive yet nourishing and that would keep well so no leftovers
would ever be wasted.

Rellenos de papas was the perfect solution. They're a
Puerto Rican tradition: potato balls filled with meat and
cheese and then fried to crispy perfection. Not only are they
delicious, but they can be made in abundance and freeze
well. Feel like mixing up the flavor? It's as easy as adding a
different seasoning to the meat while it cooks.

1. Bring a large pot of water to a boil. Add the potatoes and boil
   over high heat for 20 minutes, or until tender.

2. Drain and mash; season to taste with salt and pepper. Allow
   to cool.

3. Once cooled, add the egg and cornstarch; mix well.

4. Using cornstarch-coated hands, take a heaping spoonful of the
   mashed potato mixture and form a small disk in your palm.

5. Add a spoonful of ground beef and a sprinkle of Cheddar
   cheese. Carefully fold the potato mixture around the meat and
   cheese to form a ball. The balls can be as big or small as
   you'd like.

6. Fill a deep skillet or deep fryer with enough vegetable oil to
   submerge the potato balls. Heat the oil until it reaches a frying
   temperature between 350° and 375°F (180° and 190°C).

7. Carefully place one or two balls at a time in the hot oil and cook over medium heat. Fry for 4 to 5 minutes, or until the balls attain a golden brown color, then flip and repeat on the other side.

8. Remove from the oil; blot any excess oil on paper towels. Repeat with the remaining portions.

SYLVIA MUÑOZ

(aka Jezebel Romo and Alacrana Plata)

 AZUZA, CA • **JANUARY 2004**

WHETHER SHE IS known as Jezebel Romo, ringside manager to some of the most dastardly luchadores in LA in the mid-2000s, or by her real name, wife and business partner to Joey "Kaos" Muñoz (himself a wrestling star in XPW and Wrestling Society X), Sylvia Muñoz has played important roles in the SoCal scene.

Sylvia was born in 1971; her parents divorced before she was five years old. She would spend time with her father on weekends, which would include watching Roller Derby followed by World Wrestling Federation (WWF) wrestling—and she absolutely loved it. As she grew older, her mother became a flight attendant and her dad would stay over, sometimes for a few weeks at a time. Coming from a Mexican family, to Sylvia this also meant feeling a responsibility for taking care of her dad and brother, so she started to watch her mom, grandpa, and grandma make enchiladas, tacos, and Spanish rice, among other dishes. By trial and

error, she started making dishes that turned out to be quite edible for a nine-year-old chef.

While in high school, Sylvia outgrew both wrestling and cooking and started living what she describes as a troubled life. To try to get back on the straight and narrow, in 1993 she enlisted in the US Army. While stationed at Ft. Bragg, she had an amazing group of friends for whom she loved to cook. The problem was that in the mid-'90s, there was no Amazon and finding all the best Mexican ingredients in the middle of North Carolina was not exactly easy, so Sylvia had to get creative and began experimenting. She discovered that even though she was a finicky, picky eater (she cites her disregard for cheese as an example), she could still throw together a pretty awesome Mexican meal. "Thank God, they sold chorizo in North Carolina!" she said.

In 2001, Sylvia was back in Los Angeles and working as a receptionist when she landed at a company called Xtreme Pro Wrestling. It ran live events at the historic Grand Olympic Auditorium and Sylvia began moonlighting on the weekends as the company's "merch girl," managing official product sales at the live events. That's when her love for pro wrestling came rushing back, but this time she was not content enough just to watch—this time she wanted to *do*. Soon, she was training under Dynamite D and Angel at the XPW Asylum training school.

Unfortunately, she was let go from the receptionist job and with it, she left the Asylum. It was then that she discovered another SoCal school called the Rudos Dojo, which also ran live events under the name Rev Pro. With a little more training under her belt, Rev Pro wanted to make her a ringside manager, which launched a career now almost twenty years long. In that time, as "Jezebel Romo," Sylvia has worked in main event matches in arenas from Los Angeles to Tijuana and with legends including Mil Máscaras, Rey Misterio Sr., Misterioso, La Parka, Super Parka, and Psychosis.

Without a doubt, the most important person in Sylvia's life that she would ever manage would turn out to be the Rock Superstar Joey Kaos. The two became an inseparable duo, traveling the country trying to make a full-time living as wrestling talent. After about three years, it really felt like things were just not going to get much bigger than they were. XPW had ceased operations in 2003 and by the time Kaos and Sylvia returned to LA, SoCal hardcore wrestling legend Angel (the same Angel who had initially started training Sylvia back at the Asylum) was bugging Joey about training a group of

newbies in a real wrestling ring, but in a backyard.

Eventually he said yes and in 2008, Santino Bros. Wrestling Academy was born. These newbies became the first official class and now, more than a decade later, the SBWA is one of the most prestigious schools in the country with graduates signed to nearly every major wrestling promotion or TV series including WWE, Ring of Honor, Major League Wrestling, *Lucha Underground*, and *Championship Wrestling from Hollywood*.

Lucha libre has played a huge role in Sylvia's personal life as well; she and Kaos got married right in the middle of a Lucha VaVOOM show immediately following their match. The duo were later able to travel the world together, along with some of their SBWA graduates, after TOOL front man Maynard James Keenan was looking for a lucha-themed opening act for his side project Puscifer's tour. It was from that request that both the act Luchafer and another alter ego for Sylvia, the masked Alacrana Plata ("Silver Scorpion"), was born. "I love my mask; I love my character. It has been a blast being a sultry luchadora and I hope to be in this business for many years to come," she has been quoted as saying.

Although it was finding herself as the receptionist for a wrestling company that brought back her love for the industry, it was getting married that brought back her love for cooking. However, getting older, she has made adjustments to some of her go-to recipes, such as swapping egg roll wrappers for tortillas in an attempt to make fried foods at least a little more healthy. Whether in the wrestling ring or the kitchen, Sylvia loves passing on her knowledge.

SPANISH RICE

MAKES
4 to 6
servings

1 tablespoon (15 ml) corn oil

1 cup (195 g) uncooked white rice

1 (8-ounce [226 g]) can tomato
sauce

1 teaspoon (6.25 g) kosher salt

1 teaspoon (2 g) freshly ground
black pepper

1 teaspoon (5.6 g) garlic salt

If you're facing the dreaded dilemma of choosing the perfect side dish, Spanish rice is pretty much always a solid solution. It's tasty, cost effective, easy to make, and naturally vegan—what's not to love?

According to Sylvia Muñoz, co-owner of Santino Bros. Wrestling Academy and not-so-secret identity of luchadora Alacrana Plata, it's a bona fide crowd-pleaser: "Every time I have made this for people, they always want the recipe." She used to watch her *abuelita* [grandmother] Carmen and her own mother make it, and now it's a part of her regular repertoire.

1. In a 10- to 12-inch (25.5 to 30.5 cm) skillet with a lid, heat the oil and rice over high heat, stirring constantly, for 3 to 4 minutes, or until the rice begins to brown.

2. Add the tomato sauce, 1 cup (240 ml) of water, and the seasonings and mix to combine.

3. Bring the mixture to a boil, then cover and lower the heat to low. Cook for about 20 minutes, or until the water is completely absorbed. Serve hot.

See Sylvia's Chicken Chorizo Chimichangas on page 86 and her Skinny Tequila Sunrise on page 291.

CHECK
PAGE
86
for
Sylvia's
chimichanga recipe*

STEP ONE HEAT OIL & RICE.

Featuring

MAINS

GUADALUPE RAMIREZ

 FROM **TEPIC, NAYARIT, MEXICO**

IN MEXICO IN the 1950s, being a single mother at the age of fourteen was a lot harder than it is today. Norma Herrera López had to work and figure out how to support her kids. In those days, there were not many choices for women, so she started working in restaurants. She was very talented in the kitchen and had thoughts about opening up a restaurant of her own.

"Trust me, my grandmother could outcook any other Mexican grandmother," her grandson and proprietor of Golden Era Lucha Tees, Adrian Salas, says.

Norma opened up a small hole-in-the-wall restaurant in La Zona Norte in Tijuana, Mexico, called Los Dos Arbolitos. Next to it was a gym called La Arena Javier Escobedo, founded by Black Nasel, where luchadores would train. The luchadores would come there and eat, and Norma would watch them train. That was where she got *el gusanito*—the itch to wrestle. And so she began to train.

She would end up meeting El Cadete, a very charismatic ladies' man who would later become known as Terremoto Quintero, one of the baddest rudos in Tijuana and Los Angeles in the '70s and '80s. The two would go to matches together at the legendary Arena Danubio Azul. In the era when luchadores would go to a "territory" and stay for six months as a featured star, it was there she met Dorrel Dixon, Mil Máscaras, Black Shadow, and El Santo.

Norma started wrestling as La Loba (essentially "The She-wolf"). Terremoto Quintero said she was in great shape—as good as the male luchadores or better. As she started wrestling on live shows, she would sometimes have to take her youngest child, her son, with her. On one rare day, she took her eldest, her daughter, to a match, and when she saw her mom going up to the ring, she had a panic attack and fainted. When her daughter came to, she made her mother promise never to wrestle again.

Lucha libre had provided an escape for Norma and she knew she still wanted to be part of the whole lucha world. Lucky for her, Falcon de Oro, whom she had met in Tijuana, lived in Los Angeles and wanted to bring lucha libre to the States. Norma did whatever she could to help. She would hang out at the now legendary Gil's Garage, an LA body shop that served after hours as a gym for luchadores. She would let luchadores stay with her and her family, always cooking for them.

Over time, she became great friends with legendary Los Angeles luchador El Moro, and he became the godfather of her then youngest child, Lourdes. Norma would drive the luchadores to different arenas, such as the famed Grand Olympic Auditorium, and even drove Los Jaliscos over 1,500 miles, all the way to Guadalajara, Mexico, to make their professional debut. On these drives, her son and El Moro's often played in the backseat. El Moro's son, affectionately called YoYo at the time, would grow up to become the luchador Super Boy (see his family story and recipe on pages 152–155).

In 1978, she met a young luchador named Juan Zesati and the two moved in together. Zesati, a short but very acrobatic performer, would become best known as Super Astro. He was one of the most influential luchadores of the 1980s, helping to revolutionize the junior heavyweight high flying style and inspire a generation of luchadores led by Rey Misterio Jr., the first luchador ever to become

WWE World Champion. Rey himself has, in turn, inspired so many of today's top luchadores.

In Los Angeles, Norma owned a shop named Palace Beauty Supply, where luchadores would sometimes buy accessories for their gear. Eventually, she expanded the store and changed the name to Super Astro's Beauty Shop. The name was not a good fit for a beauty shop, especially for one located in South-Central Los Angeles. Although that business may not have been a long-term vision for her and her family, the restaurant industry had always been in her heart.

With lucha libre still extremely popular in Tijuana, and Astro now a star there, the family moved to San Diego. Feeling as if she was starting life all over again, Norma changed her name to Guadalupe and began the most influential stage of her life and career as a restaurateur and lucha libre promoter. She opened her first US restaurant, the lucha libre–themed Puerto Vallarta, in San Diego. Then, in Tijuana, she opened a second Puerto Vallarta restaurant along with a hotel next to it. She also opened up a beauty shop/boutique.

What came next would be her most influential role in the lucha libre business—becoming the first female promoter in Tijuana history by starting her own promotion (league), Promociones Internacionales. Her philosophy was a bit different than most promoters: Rather than focus on traditional star power, she wanted to focus on having the best matches because she had the most skillful luchadores. She would have mandatory meetings with the talent behind the boutique every Monday, and the luchadores had to train the Tuesday and Thursday before or they would not be given a match on her show.

At the time, Mora's "Mora y Asociados" events in Tijuana were extremely hot. Rabid, sellout crowds would pack the Auditorio de Tijuana. Norma did not flinch—she wanted to go head-to-head: Mora's star power versus her more skilled performers (if you asked her). She referred to them as *La crema y nata de lal lucha libre en Tijuana*—the cream of the cream of lucha libre in Tijuana!

Later, she would also be the first promoter to bring the brand-new Lucha Libre AAA promotion, filled with many of the country's biggest-name stars, such as Perro Aguayo, Octagón, Fuerza Guerrera, and Konnan, to Tijuana.

As influential as her legacy was in the lucha business, she also had a lasting impact on lucha-themed restaurants. (See Super Astro's story and recipe on pages 138–142.)

Just as Guadalupe's lucha libre legacy has lasted and her stories have been shared among her family and friends, so, too, have her recipes.

ALBONDIGAS SOUP

SERVES
4 to 6

1 tablespoon (15 ml) vegetable oil

1 large onion, diced

1 large tomato, diced

2 tablespoons (24 g) chicken
bouillon powder

5 ounces (140 g) canned tomato
sauce

2 pounds (905 g) ground beef

⅓ cup (65 g) uncooked rice

2 large eggs

¼ cup (10 g) fresh cilantro leaves,
finely chopped

¼ cup (15 g) fresh parsley, finely
chopped

1 teaspoon (1 g) dried oregano

1½ to 2 tablespoons (22 to 29 g)
Lawry's Seasoned Salt to taste

½ teaspoon (1 g) freshly ground
black pepper

3 large carrots, cut into thirds
(cylinder shaped)

2 large potatoes, cut into quarters
(peeled or unpeeled to your
preference)

2 large green zucchini, cut into
¼-inch (6 mm)-thick coins

When he was young, Adrian Salas's mother was frequently out of the house working, so he often stayed with his grandma—but this wasn't your average granny. Guadalupe Ramirez was also the first woman in the area to become a lucha promoter in Tijuana, eventually working her way to become one of the most important promoters in the city's history. Her influence was not only felt in the lucha scene but in related restaurants too. She started a number of different establishments with Adrian's grandfather, Super Astro.

Grandma Guadalupe originally learned how to make albondigas, an aromatic meatball soup, from her mother, Sylvia. Over the years, she adapted it in a variety of ways—most notably with the addition of Lawry's Seasoned Salt. While watching Adrian, she'd make this recipe a lot—to the point that he became thoroughly tired of it! But these days, his grandmother's absence has made his heart grow fonder for this dish.

It's easy to make this recipe your own: Want to up the salt and pepper? Go for it. Want to add a different spice or some different veggies? You do you!

1. In a large pot over low heat, combine the oil and about one-third each of the onion and tomato. Fry until the onion has lightly browned, about 3 minutes.

2. Add 3 cups (710 ml) of water and the chicken bouillon powder. Next, add one-third of the tomato sauce. Bring the mixture to a boil.

3. Meanwhile, make the albondigas (meatballs): In a large bowl, combine the ground beef, rice, eggs, remaining onion and tomato, cilantro, parsley, oregano, Lawry's Seasoned Salt, and pepper.

4. Mix well by hand, then form into meatballs (the size is up to you). Add the meatballs to the pot.

5. Add the carrots, potatoes, and zucchini, then cover. Bring the heat to medium low and cook for 45 minutes to 1 hour. To check doneness, use a spoon to check the texture of the vegetables; they should be soft enough that they can be easily cut. The rice in the meatballs should appear fluffy and plump.

6. Using a spoon, skim off any oil that may have accumulated on the surface of the soup; serve hot.

What's Lawry's Seasoned Salt?

This popular seasoning includes salt and aromatics, herbs, and spices, including garlic, onion, paprika, and turmeric. It's one of those "put this on everything" types of seasonings!

HIJO DEL PERRO AGUAYO

 MEXICO CITY, MEXICO ✦ **JUNE 1995**

FTEN, WE HEAR people are born to do something. Pedro Aguayo Ramirez, better known as Hijo del Perro Aguayo, was born to be a luchador. As a son of arguably Mexico's biggest box office attractions, Perro Aguayo (Pedro Aguayo Damián), he was destined to follow in his father's footsteps. Just before his sixteenth birthday, he made his debut in grand fashion before nearly twenty thousand fans for one of the largest wrestling companies in the world, on that company's biggest event of the year.

Asistencia Asesoría y Administración (AAA)'s Triplemanía is the company's biggest event, its WrestleMania. On June 18, 1995, at Rio Nilo Coliseum in Tonalá Jalisco, Hijo del Perro Aguayo made his debut showing a ton of potential, losing an Olympic-style match to another second-generation sensation, Juventud Guerrera. A week before his birthday, he made his US debut at the LA Sports Arena, once again facing Guerrera as nearly nine thousand fans watched.

Over the next few years, "Perrito," as the younger Aguayo was often called, wrestled across Mexico and the southern United States. Some fans in the US may remember his brief nontelevised appearance at the 1997 WWF Royal Rumble, where he teamed with Venum to defeat Mosco de la Merced and Maniaco in front of sixty thousand fans at the Alamo Dome in San Antonio, Texas. Not many seventeen-year-old kids have wrestled in front of over sixty thousand fans for the largest wrestling company in the world.

While Hijo del Perro Aguayo was proving himself in AAA, his father returned to Consejo Mundial de Lucha Libre (CMLL). With Aguayo Sr., seasoned veterans, and a mix of young wrestlers coming into their own, business started increasing for CMLL. His return to Arena México was part of an announced retirement tour, as he wanted to finish his career with the company where he first found fame some thirty years earlier. Father and son continued working for rival promotions until the summer of 2003.

On August 1, 2003, Perrito arrived in the building where his father had so many classic battles over the years—the famed Arena México. CMLL had seen its share of highs and lows; in the mid-1990s, the company reached one of its lowest periods at the box office, but by the early 2000s, it had regained its composure and was on the upswing. Aguayo made an immediate impact upon his return. Just six weeks after his return on September 19, 2003, during the company's seventieth anniversary, he teamed with Negro Casas to capture the CMLL Tag Team Championship from Los Guerreros del Infierno.

The year 2004 was an even bigger year for CMLL and Hijo del Perro Aguayo. Featured at a June 18, 2004, event honoring the thirtieth anniversary of El Satánico was a multiperson cage match where the loser would have their hair shaved. The finale came down to Perrito pinning his partner, the legendary Negro Casas, and taking his hair. This event would foreshadow the younger Aguayo's run as a *rudo* (bad guy). It also featured the appearance of one of Perro's best rivals and a future box office champion, Místico. A week later, the return of his longtime friend Hector Garza would set the stage for one of Mexico's famous factions.

Aguayo soon found himself having problems (story line ones) with his tag-team partner Negro Casas, which culminated at the annual Leyenda de Plata tournament. In the finals of the tournament, Aguayo defeated El Felino to capture the Leyenda de Plata trophy. During the closing ceremony, El Hijo del Santo, the son of the man honored, came out to present the trophy to Perro Aguayo Jr., which offended him. He stated he didn't want a trophy honoring El Hijo del Santo, as he felt his father was the true legend. He then viciously attacked Santo with his trophy, to the shock of the fans! These events led to Perrito and partner Damián el Terrible joining forces with Hector Garza, calling themselves La Furia del Norte.

Business was booming. Friday night events at Arena México were selling out consistently with scalpers buying up tickets so fast that it became a business all unto its own. Two reasons for the increase in business were the explosion in popularity of Místico and the formation of one of the most successful heel groups in all of wrestling: Perros del Mal.

Although Perros del Mal may have started off as a spin-off of La Furia del Norte with the original members Hijo del Perro Aguayo, Hector Garza, Tarzan Boy, and Damián el Terrible, the group quickly became the number one rudo combination in all of Mexico. Perros del Mal merchandise became a hot item. Every night, you could look out and witness a sea of people wearing Perros del Mal T-shirts. Soon after, celebrities and other famous athletes started wearing the shirts. Much like how the "NWO" from World Championship Wrestling broke through to become US pop culture in the mid-'90s, Perros del Mal became Mexican pop culture.

As successful as Perro's time in CMLL was, it only lasted five years. Perros del Mal was a major reason for the company's success. To continue the momentum, a story line was devised for Perros del Mal to become independent. On the surface, Perros del Mal would become its own promoter and engage with rivals from CMLL. In reality, it would work alongside CMLL, eventually doing an interpromotion angle. However, what started as a story line turned into reality when Los Perros del Mal Producciones was founded. It broke out on its own as completely independent, but on June 6, 2010, Perros del Mal made a dramatic appearance at AAA's Triplemanía, Mexico's largest lucha libre event of the year. The PDM faction formed a partnership with Konnan (see page 70) and AAA owner Dorian Roldán to form a group called La Sociedad, which became the top rudos group in the company.

In the early part of 2010, Perro started experiencing extreme pain in his abdomen. At first he thought he had broken a rib, but after he checked himself into the hospital, he found out it was more serious than that. With his health problems being shielded from the media, Perro underwent surgery to remove a tumor in his stomach. Rumors were spreading and at the time there was concern this could end his in-ring career or, worse, be life-threatening. During a press conference a few months later, Perro stated he had a cancerous tumor removed from his stomach and had undergone chemotherapy, which explained his hair loss. He went on to say his doctors expected a full recovery; however, he would have to wear a girdle when he wrestled, and to change his diet dramatically.

When he came back, it was obvious it had taken a toll on him physically. Even with his limitations, he continued to be a great performer and few could match his off-the-chart charisma. On March 18, 2012, he took part in AAA's annual event: Rey de Reyes. He faced LA Park, Jack Evans, and personal friend Hector Garza in the Rey de Reyes elimination tournament, where he walked away as the winner.

For the next five years, Perros del Mal, both as its own promotion and as a rotating lineup of Perros del Mal faction members in AAA, remained one of the hottest acts in Mexico, but on Friday, March 20, 2015, tragedy struck.

It was meant to be a huge homecoming celebration as Rey Mysterio returned to the building where he started his wrestling career, the famous Auditorio de Tijuana. Rey teamed with another luchador who broke in at the same place: Extreme Tiger. The duo faced off with Hijo del Perro Aguayo and his partner Manik, aka TJ Perkins (see page 156). In an extreme freak accident, Perrito suffered a life-threatening injury in the match, and by the time he was at the hospital, there was no chance to save him.

Pedro Aguayo Ramirez lived to the age of thirty-five and spent more than half those years as a luchador. Much like his father, who ascended to being the country's biggest técnico, the younger Aguayo is also at the top of that list, though as the industry's biggest rudo. But it was Perrito and his Perros del Mal faction that made being a rudo cool. The Perros del Mal brand still lives on today, both as a faction within Lucha Libre AAA and in branded merchandise sold throughout the globe.

ARROZ A LA PERROS DEL MAL

SERVES
4

- 2 cups (400 g) uncooked sushi rice
- 2 large eggs
- 2 (5g) packets pickled sushi ginger (10g)
- 1½ teaspoons (7.5 ml) olive oil
- 4 ounces (115 g) finely cut beef
- 1 surimi (imitation crabmeat) bar
- 4 tablespoons (60 ml) eel sauce, katsu sauce, or Bull-Dog Sauce, or to taste

1. Prepare the rice in a rice steamer or, if you don't have a rice steamer, combine the rice with 4 cups (946 ml) of water in a saucepan. Bring to a boil, then cook, covered, over low heat for 20 to 25 minutes. When the rice is nearly done, crack the two eggs on top so that the steam will cook them.
2. Rinse the ginger to dilute the flavor.
3. In a large skillet, heat the olive oil and fry the ginger for 2 minutes, or until a bit golden. Remove the ginger from the pan and cut it into small pieces. Do not rinse the pan.
4. In the same pan, fry the beef for 3 minutes, then add the surimi and cook for 1 more minute, just to warm up.
5. Once done, remove and mince the meat and surimi.
6. Place the ginger, minced meat and surimi, rice, and eggs in the pan and stir. Add the eel sauce.

SOLAR AND SOLAR JR.

SOLAR:

 ZACOALCO DE TORRES, JALISCO, MEXICO ✦ MAY 1975

SOLAR JR.:

 MEXICO CITY, MEXICO ✦ MAY 2015

SOLAR IS ONE of only a handful of luchadores who have had a long career in the sport, and has retained his mask and identity for more than forty-five years. This means that much of his real identity is private. Over the past five decades, he has not only helped to usher in exciting new eras, but he is also seen as one of the technical masters of lucha libre—one of very few luchadores to be referred to as a *maestro de maestros* (a teacher of teachers).

Solar began his career in May 1975 in San Luis Potosí, making his debut suddenly when a wrestler unexpectedly did not show up to an event. Prior to that, Solar had been training as a luchador with Toño Cruz and the brother team known as Los Calaveras I and II. As a young man, Solar had trained in amateur grappling; in exchange for teaching his trainers Olympic style, or "real wrestling," they would teach him the art of lucha libre.

Another trainer Solar has credited with his success is the legendary Diablo Velazco, a hall of fame trainer who even skilled luchadores seek out to learn from and who has been credited with training some of the biggest names in the history of the sport.

It was apparent from the start that Solar was highly skilled, as just a few years into his career, he gained the reputation for his on-the-mat skills and highly technical submission holds he would implement during matches. Early in his career, he was brought into the UWA promotion run by Francisco Flores and Benjamin Mora. Originally called Lucha Libre Internacional at the time, it was one of the most successful wrestling companies, not just in Mexico, but in the entire world.

One of Solar's first major singles matches took place May 29, 1977, at the enormous Palacio de los Deportes in Mexico when he dethroned Villano III to become only the second UWA World Welterweight Champion. While the championships were new titles, the Universal Wrestling Association (UWA) promotion, with its international connections to New Japan Pro-Wrestling and World Wide Wrestling Federation (WWWF, the predecessor to the WWF), the titles quickly became very desirable championships to wrestlers from around the globe.

Solar would go on to hold this title for a year before losing it to Bobby Lee on July 16, 1978, at Plaza de Toros el Monumental in Monterrey. It was there in Monterrey for promoter Rene Guajardo where Solar gained a lot of his early notoriety, which opened the doors for him to go to the larger UWA promotion in Mexico City.

Soon his brother would join him, taking the name Solar II, wearing similar mask and ring gear. To avoid confusion, Solar would often appear as Solar I. It was not uncommon for the brothers to appear in matches together. Solar also shared the ring with numerous famous luchadores as tag team partners early in his career. He could be seen teaming with such legends as El Solitario, Anibal, Dos Caras, Tinieblas Sr., Rayo de Jalisco, and Dorrel Dixon. Teaming with top técnicos helped establish Solar as one of Mexico's brightest young stars.

On December 9, 1979, at Palacio de los Deportes in Mexico City, Solar would put up his mask against the hood of Dr. O'Borman in a "lucha de apuestas" match. Solar came out the victor that evening, scoring one of the biggest masks earlier in his career.

A few more championships came to Solar at the hands of rival Cachorro Mendoza. The first took place at the finals of the historic Mexican National Middleweight Championship tournament on May 29, 1981, at Arena Coliseo. The second title taken from Mendoza took place on November 20, 1985, in the main event at El Toreo de Cuatro Caminos in Naucalpan, when he won the UWA World Middleweight Championship.

When trios wrestling exploded in the early 1980s, Solar was a major part of the attraction. Teaming with partners Super Astro and Ultraman, they formed a unit called Los Cadetes del Espacio. The Space Cadets became instant fan favorites with their high-flying matches. They would battle trios, such as Hall of Fame team Los Misioneros de la Muerte (El Signo, El Texano, and Negro Navarro); or Los Temararios, Los Brazos, Los Exoticos; or the team that was possibly their biggest rival of the era, the trio of Kato Kung Lee, Black Man, and Kung Fu—Los Fantasticos.

It was Los Fantasticos that defeated Los Cadetes del Espacio on March 18, 1984, at El Toreo de Cautro Caminos in Naucalpan, to capture the first ever UWA World Trios Championships. After numerous opportunities, it was a championship the Cadets were never able to capture. They did capture the hairs of Los Temararios during a trios apuestas match. It took place on July 8, 1984, at El Toreo, when they placed their masks against the hair of Black Terry, Jose Luis Feliciano, and El Lobo Rubio in front of a near-full house of more than fifteen thousand fans at the bullring!

When UWA closed, Solar moved over to Asistencia Asesoría y Administración (now Lucha Libre AAA) and, in something of a surprise, began wrestling under a new name and new outfit, now calling himself El Mariachi. He would come to the ring playing the trumpet and wearing a sombrero and attempted to create a whole new persona. It didn't last long, and he would soon return to competing under his more famous name and moved on to work for the Consejo Mundial de Lucha Libre. In the 2000s, he was also featured in the short-lived Lucha Libre USA show that ran for two seasons on MTV2.

Solar and his Los Cadetes partner Super Astro are the stars of their own modern-day comic book as part of The Luchaverse. Solar & Super Astro: Los Cadetes del Espacio places them in a shared comic book universe with legends Rey Mysterio, Konnan, Tinieblas Jr., and today's most popular luchadores on the planet—the Lucha Brothers Penta Zero M and Rey Fenix.

The legend has his own store, Tienda Solar, in Mexico City, where most weeks he holds in-store meet-and-greets with other legendary luchadores and lucha libre personalities. If you are ever in Mexico, it is only a few minutes from Arena México, the top tourist spot for catching a lucha libre event.

Solar continues to compete on the independent scene, often in Maestro matches, with other veteran luchadores. The Solar legacy continues today with his son, Solar Jr. The heir to the iconic mask with the sun, Solar Jr. began wrestling at events in 2008, though, like many second-generation luchadores, he did not begin using his father's name until he had been deemed worthy.

This would come one short year later, in 2009. Father and son will often team up against other legendary lucha families and Solar Jr. has had his share of feuds with other juniors, including Fishman Jr. He has battled—and is probably destined to forever be locked in an eternal conflict—with Los Traumas, the sons of his father's most hated rival, Negro Navarro. In fact, there is even an animated series, in development by Masked Republic, which brings the family rivalry into a whole new animated world.

AZTEC CAKE
(AKA LASAGNA SOLAR)

SERVES
4

9 ounces (255 g) boneless, skinless chicken breast

½ medium-size white onion, chopped

4 garlic cloves, halved

6 bay leaves

1 teaspoon (0.6 g) dried marjoram

1 teaspoon (0.8 g) fresh thyme

Kosher salt

4 Roma tomatoes

1 teaspoon (2 g) freshly ground black pepper

Cooking spray, for baking dish

15 white corn tortillas

15 slices Mexican Manchego or Chihuahua cheese

Tradition is a big part of luchador Solar's life. He's been a luchador for more than forty-five years and he's passed on the tradition to his son Solar Jr., who is also a noted luchador in his own right.

But a love for lucha isn't the only thing he's shared with his son. Solar has also passed down plenty of cooking lessons over the years, and this recipe is a family favorite. The name is something of a misnomer: Aztec cake is actually more of a casserole, composed of gooey layers of chicken, homemade salsa, and cheese. It's not hard to see why they refer to it as Lasagna Solar in their household.

1. In a medium-size pot, combine the chicken, half of the chopped onion, three of the garlic cloves (six halves), bay leaves, marjoram, thyme, and salt.

2. Add water until the chicken is completely submerged and let boil for 30 minutes over medium heat, or until the interior of the chicken is no longer pink and its internal temperature is 165°F (74°C). Remove from the heat; drain, reserving a ½ cup (120 ml) of the broth for later use. Once cooled, shred the chicken; set aside.

3. In a second medium-size pot, cover the tomatoes with 2 cups (475 ml) of water. Boil for 20 minutes over medium heat, then drain and let cool.

GOOEY LAYERS OF *chicken, salsa & cheese*

STEP TWO BOIL THE TOMATOES.

4. Remove the skin and seeds from the tomatoes. Transfer to a blender; blend with the remaining onion, remaining garlic cloves (2 halves), pepper, and the reserved broth from boiling the chicken.

5. Preheat the oven to 350°F (180°C).

6. Spray a 10 x 15-inch (25.5 x 38 cm) glass baking dish with cooking spray. Spread the tomato sauce along the bottom of the dish, then cover with three to four tortillas. Add a layer of shredded chicken and cheese, then top with more tomato sauce. Repeat these layers three more times, reserving a final layer of cheese for the top of the casserole.

7. Bake until the cheese has melted, for 20 to 25 minutes. Remove from the oven and let cool slightly before serving.

PALEHORSE & MONSTER GO TO MEXICO

Sometime in 2014, an idea was born that would quickly become the most expansive creative undertaking of my life. After regularly attending indie wrestling shows in Tampa for a few months with digital illustrator Chris Parks (aka Palehorse), we began discussing the possibility of creating our own luchador characters and somehow convincing a few wrestlers to perform as these characters sometime in the future. Even though it was just a rough concept at the time, we both felt that it was worth exploring and began working on what would later be known as Palehorse Lucha.

After long nights brainstorming at the studio, Chris would produce sketches based on the ideas and concepts we'd discussed, and I would use those sketches as inspiration to draft the mythology of the luchador characters. Working in almost total isolation and secrecy for over a year allowed us to fully immerse ourselves in the world we were constructing.

The existing frameworks of pro wrestling and lucha libre were the furthest things from our mind during this process. Instead, our frames of reference were ancient myths, forgotten history, science fiction, obscure religious texts, fringe podcasts, and late-night AM radio shows about UFOs, Bigfoot, and the supernatural. Nothing was ever too weird or out of bounds for us to draw inspiration from.

The Palehorse Lucha project would eventually result in two sold-out gallery shows in 2015 and 2016, featuring original artwork by Chris and lucha libre—themed music, videos, and photography by local artist friends, who generously lent their talents to assist us in realizing our vision. It also featured live in-ring performances by luchadores portraying the six characters we created.

But that isn't the story being told here. The real question is: How do two Florida-based artists, who incidentally don't speak a single word of Spanish between them, end up in Mexico City having dinner at the home of legendary lucha libre star Solar?

Through one of the luchadores we were working with on the Palehorse Lucha project, we had been put in touch with US-based lucha merchandising and production company Masked Republic. Co-owner Kevin Kleinrock suggested that we reach out to his business partner, Ruben Zamora, about setting up a visit to Mexico. When Ruben invited us to accompany him on his upcoming trip to Mexico City to meet with some of the most storied figures in Mexican wrestling history and take in a long weekend of lucha libre shows, it was obvious that we had to go.

For over forty years, Solar has been one of the most recognizable and well-respected figures in all of lucha libre. In addition to a very successful singles career, Solar may be best remembered as a third of the futuristic trio known as Los Cadetes del Espacio (The Space Cadets), along with Super Astro and Ultraman.

Our first outing after arriving in Mexico City was a journey with Solar to Teotihuacan for a tour of the Pyramids of the Sun and Moon. The Pyramid of the Sun is incredibly steep and over a half-mile (0.8 km) tall, which didn't faze the well-conditioned luchador, as he insisted on jogging to the top. After acting as our tour guide and chauffeur for the day, Solar insisted that we come to his home for dinner, an offer we were more than happy to accept.

Chris was formally welcomed to casa de Solar with a large chalice of beer and a giant plate of chicken. Solar quickly noticed that I didn't have any chicken on my plate and that my glass was full of hibiscus tea, not milk or beer as he was drinking. When I explained through Ruben that I'm a vegetarian, Solar buried his face deep in his hands and shook his head in despair. He said, "You need to drink milk and eat meat! How else will you ever have the body of a wrestler?" In all fairness, Solar did have a pretty valid point. Fortunately, Solar's wife didn't feel the same need to fatten me up for a career in lucha libre, and she prepared for me an incredible dish of vegetables, rice, and a large piece of grilled cactus that she cut from a plant in her backyard.

After a five-course meal, we sat around the dinner table and shared sketches of our stable of Palehorse Lucha characters with Solar and his family; they were well received. Despite the language barrier, our mask and costume designs effectively conveyed the stories of the luchadores to our hosts and led to some wonderful conversations about the deeper meaning of lucha libre itself. Looking back years later, it was a surreal experience made possible only by dedicating ourselves to a vision that seemed impossible to ever fully realize.

Not only was our vision realized in the Palehorse Lucha projects, but we exceeded our own expectations and connected with people around the world who continue to inspire us and our work to this day.

And while I may never have the body of a wrestler, I will always have my dinner with Solar.

—MONSTER

LEFT TO RIGHT: PALEHORSE, SOLAR, MONSTER

ÓSCAR GARCÍA JIMÉNEZ

 MEXICO CITY, MEXICO

WHEN WATCHING LUCHA libre, you'll notice the cool characters and impressive outfits, along with the backstory of the luchadores' characters. Some characters have extremely extensive backgrounds surrounding them. For second-generation creative mind Óscar García Jiménez, it started like many—becoming a fan first.

Óscar would watch lucha libre with his father, who would later work for Antonio Peña in the early years of AAA. As a kid, he was introduced to Peña, whom Óscar admired because he was highly creative. Óscar always looked up to Peña as a lucha libre version of Walt Disney. Once when he was young, Óscar presented Antonio with an art toy he made for him and Antonio was impressed, telling the young Óscar, "I know that one day you'll work here."

Unfortunately, Peña passed away before Óscar was able to start with the company, but the legendary promoter's premonition was right. He would go on to work for AAA alongside some of the company's biggest stars, by creating or designing characters or costumes for them.

Often that creative process begins with a meeting with Dorian Roldán or Konnan, who likes to change the character of a young luchador in hopes it will increase their popularity. He'll sit down with the luchadores and learn a little about their personalities and collaborate on some ideas before going all out on working on the designs. He has also added elements—for example, body paint—to help the characters leave an impression on the fans.

You can see some of Óscar's work with such luchadores as Pentagón Jr. (aka Penta Zero M), Rey Fenix, Drago, Australian Suicide, Taurus, Lady Shani, Parka Negra, Jack Evans, Angelico, Chessman, and many more.

AZTEC SOUP

SERVES
1

2 medium-size tomatoes

2 cascabel chiles

1 small white onion, chopped

Kosher salt

½ cup (120 ml) vegetable oil (may need slightly more or less)

2 corn tortillas, cut into strips

1 pasilla chile, julienned

TO SERVE:

2 tablespoons (30 g) sour cream

3.5 ounces (about 100 g) panela cheese, diced

½ ripe avocado, peeled, pitted, and diced

On a day-to-day basis, Óscar García Jiménez channels his inner Aztec warrior to design fight-ready attire and masks for some of the biggest lucha names out there. He's had a hand in creating the looks of top luchadores, including Penta Zero M, Rey Fenix, Taurus, and Drago, to name a few.

But even Aztec warriors have to eat—and this soup is the perfect fuel!

1. In a medium-size pot over medium-high heat, combine tomatoes, cascabel chiles, and onion. Add enough water to submerge the ingredients. Bring the mixture to a boil and cook for 30 minutes. Remove from heat, let cool, and add salt to taste. Using a fine strainer, strain to get rid of tomato seeds and chile skin and seeds.

2. In a second medium-size saucepan, combine 2 tablespoons (30 ml) of the oil and the strained sauce. Simmer over low heat for 30 minutes; season to taste.

3. In a third medium-size saucepan, heat about ¼ cup of oil (or enough to fry the tortillas). Fry the tortilla strips for 3 to 5 minutes, or until golden and crunchy; transfer to a paper towel to blot excess oil.

4. In the same saucepan used for the tortilla strips, heat the remaining 2 tablespoons (30 ml) of oil. Once hot, add the pasilla chile and cook for 1 to 2 minutes, or until browned. Don't cook the chile for more than 2 minutes; it can make the flavor bitter.

5. To serve, place the fried tortilla strips, sour cream, diced cheese, and avocado in a bowl; top with the pasilla chile and sauce. Serve hot.

LUCHADOR

ÚLTIMO PANDA

 FROM **JAPANDA (ALLEGEDLY)** ◆ **DEBUT** **DECEMBER 2013**

A TWENTY-PLUS-YEAR veteran, Último Panda is exactly what he sounds like—a very large panda. As adept at the lucha style as he is at making people laugh, Panda is a mainstay of the California lucha libre promotion Pro Wrestling Revolution. There, he has guarded PWR against invading forces, such as Kikutaro, Drake Younger, and Famous B, while also forming a fun tag team with IMPACT Wrestling star Willie Mack. In between all that, Panda has even found time to work a few Dragonmania shows in "the mecca of lucha libre," Arena México, for Último Dragón, as well as an event for the oldest lucha libre company on the planet, CMLL, in Guadalajara. All the more proof that the Panda is lucha libre to the bone.

FUN FACTS

★ Último Panda is a former PWR Tag Team Champion with Willie Mack.

★ In addition to CMLL, he's also competed for The Crash and the International Wrestling Revolution Group in Mexico.

★ He's thought to be popular California wrestler, Vinnie Massaro, the former *Lucha Underground* star and trainer of Cain Velasquez, under the mask, though he has vehemently denied these allegations. Still the rumors persist and will continue to until Massaro and Panda are seen together at the same time.

BAMBOO SHOOT PASTA (AGLIO E OLIO)

SERVES
4 to 6

1 pound (455 g) bamboo spaghetti (see note)

1 tablespoon (18 g) kosher salt

⅓ cup (80 ml) extra-virgin olive oil

8 garlic cloves, cut into thin slivers

½ teaspoon (1.3 g) crushed red pepper flakes

½ cup (30 g) fresh parsley, minced

1 cup (100 g) Parmesan cheese, grated, plus more for serving

Último Panda doesn't just dress like a panda; he eats like one too. Well, a very fancy panda with a penchant for Italian food, anyway. (Rumor has it this influence may have come from his dear, close personal friend and fellow luchador, Vinnie Massaro.)

At first glance, this may look like a fairly simple and run-of-the-mill pasta recipe featuring olive oil, garlic, red pepper flakes, cheese, and parsley. But the whole dish takes on new meaning when you make it with bamboo pasta! To those who aren't in the know, this unique gluten-free pasta is made with bamboo flour—because, apparently, that's a thing.

NOTES: In addition to being tasty, bamboo pasta is also a prudent pick for health-conscious luchadores: The flour is said to slow down carbohydrate absorption, and it's naturally low in calories. Panda gets his bamboo pasta online from Pasta Natura. Says Panda, "You can use regular pasta if you don't have bamboo, but then you won't have abs like I do."

Panda suggests using a really high-quality olive oil in this recipe. It makes a difference!

1. Bring a large pot of water to a boil over high heat. Add the pasta and 2 teaspoons of the salt and cook according to the directions on the package.

2. Once complete, drain the pasta, reserving 1½ cups of the cooking water.

3. Meanwhile, in a 12-inch saucepan or pot sufficient to hold the pasta, heat the olive oil over medium heat. Add the garlic and cook, stirring frequently, until it begins to turn golden on the edges, about 2 minutes; don't overcook!

4. Add the red pepper flakes; cook for 30 more seconds. Carefully add the reserved pasta-cooking water to the garlic and oil (it may splatter at first). Increase the heat and bring to a boil.

5. Once the mixture is boiling, lower the heat, add the remaining teaspoon of salt, and simmer for about 5 minutes, or until the liquid is reduced by about a third.

6. Add the drained pasta to the garlic sauce and toss. Remove from the heat; add the parsley and Parmesan and toss again. Let the pasta rest off the heat for 5 minutes to allow the sauce to be absorbed. Give it a taste and season as desired; serve warm with extra Parmesan on the side.

CALDO DE POLLO (CHICKEN SOUP)

MAKES
6
servings

About 18 ounces (500 g) chicken legs and thighs

2 green pumpkins, seeded, julienned

2 medium-size carrots, peeled and sliced

2 medium-size potatoes, peeled and sliced

1 chayote squash, seeded and sliced into 4 portions

Kosher salt and freshly ground black pepper

1 tablespoon (15 ml) chicken consommé

When luchadora Amazona suffered a knee injury and needed surgery, she needed plenty of rest…and good, healing food. Since she wasn't going to be as active for a while, weight gain was a concern, so she called up a nutritionist for help with a diet plan.

Amazona was given this recipe and adapted it to suit her needs. She ate it every night for three months until she learned that she was pregnant and had to change up her diet! She still loves this soup, but these days it's less for weight control and more because it's so easy and tasty.

NOTE: To really channel your inner luchadora while making this soup, follow Amazona's lead and sing *cumbia* songs while you cook!

1. In a medium-size pot over low heat, bring 6 cups (1.4 L) of water to a simmer.
2. Add the chicken. Cook over medium heat for 6 minutes, then add the pumpkin, carrots, potatoes, and squash. Let cook for about 15 minutes.
3. Add salt and pepper to taste, along with the chicken consommé.
4. Check with a fork that the vegetables are soft and the chicken is cooking. Cook for 20 to 25 more minutes, or until the chicken reaches an internal temperature of 165°F (73°C).
5. Serve with a *birote* or corn tortilla.

What is a birote?

This is a type of Mexican sourdough bread that's produced in Jalisco, in Guadalajara. It has the shape of a baguette but a much softer consistency, more like a *bolillo* roll.

See pages 10–12 for Amazona's story and Cheese Ball recipe.

KONNAN

 SANTIAGO DE CUBA, CUBA • **JANUARY 1987**

CARLOS SANTIAGO ESPADA Moises was born January 6, 1964, in the city of Santiago de Cuba, 45 miles (72.4 km) from Guantánamo Bay. When he was two years old, his mother, Vilma Moises Alfonso, brought Carlos to the US to give him a better life. They arrived in Boston, Massachusetts, which is where she met a young private investigator from New York named Richard Ashenoff, who was of half-Jewish, half–Puerto Rican descent; the two got married and Richard adopted Carlos, changing his legal last name to Ashenoff.

In 1967, the family relocated to South Florida, where Carlos would spend most of his youth. As a teenager, growing up in a rough part of Dade County, Carlos took to boxing and began lifting weights. After graduating from Miami Senior High School and shortly after his eighteenth birthday, Carlos was caught selling drugs. The presiding judge over the case decided to give him an option of either enlisting in the military, in hopes of rehabilitating him, or sending him to jail. Carlos chose the first option and within a week he enlisted in the US Navy.

After basic training, Carlos was stationed in San Diego and assigned to the USS *Cape Cod*. While he was stationed in San Diego, he continued to ply his trade at boxing. It was during his time training at a boxing gym when a super fan of wrestling, John Roberts, introduced himself to Carlos and convinced him that he had connections to the lucha libre promotion based in Tijuana. In 1987, John Roberts took Carlos to Auditorio Fausto Gutiérrez Moreno to introduce him to the world of lucha libre.

Auditorio Fausto Gutiérrez Moreno, also referred to as Auditorio de Tijuana, is a famous gymnasium that held weekly lucha libre events as far back as 1969. It was at the five thousand–seat auditorium where Carlos was introduced to Manuel de los Santos. Roberts, claiming to be a "business manager" for wrestlers, had told de los Santos that Carlos had been wrestling in Florida to get him booked for that evening's event. After being introduced to de los Santos, Carlos came clean and told Manuel that he in fact had no training. Overhearing all this, Miguel López, then simply know as luchador Rey Misterio, told

Carlos that his "manager" was nothing more than a fan who was always in the front row of the shows. And with that, Carlos's career could have been over before it ever began.

However, it was obvious that de los Santos was impressed with Carlos's look and physique, which was very large for Mexican wrestling standards. López and de los Santos convinced Carlos to step into the ring that night to give it a try. He was given a mask and introduced to the crowd as El Centurion and made quick work of his opponent. It was a very impressive debut to the fans at the auditorium.

Shortly after, Carlos began officially training under López in the famed Gimnasio de Tijuana, which is located behind the Auditorio. Others who were training for lucha libre at the time were Dionicio Castellanos and the young nephew of Miguel López, Óscar Gutiérrez. They would go on to gain worldwide fame as Psychosis and Rey Mysterio!

After training and gaining some experience wrestling as El Centurion and the Incredible Hulk, Carlos was given the name Conan el Barbaro and had his official debut on his twenty-fourth birthday. Wrestling as Conan, his name was tweaked depending on the company; he was working with different variations of that name until finally settling on the name Konnan, or Konnan El Bárbaro.

Konnan's popularity in the country grew quickly, first becoming a top attraction in the Tijuana territory, to moving to the even larger Juárez territory, where he became friends with the famous Guerrero family and close friends and partners with the youngest son, Eddie Guerrero. The Juárez territory turned into a red-hot promotion drawing numerous sellout crowds twice a week at El Gimnasio Municipal Josué "Neri" Santos.

The territory had a local television show that was broadcast throughout the region. Add that to Konnan's national magazine coverage, and word spread quickly across Mexico of this young wrestler who was getting tremendous reactions and selling lots of tickets. This brought Konnan resentment from some of the more established wrestlers in the locker room along with attention from promoters who owned larger companies.

One of the first promoters who contacted Konnan was Monterrey promoter Carlos Elizondo. Elizondo's promotion was even bigger, and business was going well. Another promoter, Carlos Maynes, who ran one of Mexico's two largest promotions, UWA, reached out about bringing him in to the Mexico City suburb of Naucalpan to wrestle at his El Toreo de Cuatro Caminos, a bullring that Maynes ran shows in twice a week and could hold as many as eighteen thousand spectators. Konnan's name was such that he was being requested across Mexico and was being used on top of the card facing off with the biggest stars in Mexico.

In late 1989, Antonio Peña, who was working in the front office for EMLL, started pushing for Konnan to make the jump. Peña, who had only been with the company a short time, impressed owner Paco Alonso with his imagination and ability to create successful characters. It was also during this time that EMLL made a deal to air its matches on television on the country's largest network, Televisa; this was a huge deal because there had been no lucha libre on Televisa before this. Around the same time Konnan made the move and began wrestling at the famed Arena México for the oldest promotion in the world, EMLL (now CMLL). Lucha libre had been banned on television in the Distrito Federal since the mid-1950s. The combination of lucha appearing on Televisa and the introduction of new characters ushered in a tremendous boom period for the sport.

Carlos, who was still wrestling under a mask, became one of the country's biggest stars. One of Mexico's major feuds began to take shape between the young luchador Konnan and veteran Perro Aguayo. Perro was famous for his bloody brawls and the reputation he had built over the previous few decades competing inside the ring. Aguayo wrestled as both a *rudo* (bad guy) and a *técnico* (good guy); to his fans it really didn't matter, as he had gained so much respect through the years that many of his longtime fans would not boo him. In early 1991, Arena México was doing huge business, and challenges back and forth were being made for an *apuestas* (betting) match, the most important type of match in lucha libre; Konnan wanted the hair of Perro and Perro wanted the mask of Konnan!

Leading up to the match on March 22, 1991, Arena México had seen five straight sellouts. On this night, not only did the venue sell out every seat in the building, but it added temporary seating and had fans sitting in the aisles. It was said that nearly twenty thousand fans were inside Arena México that night, with another four thousand outside watching the match on big screens that were set up to avoid those fans from rushing into the building and causing damage, which had occurred the year before. That evening Konnan lost the match to Perro Aguayo and thus had to remove his mask, which endeared him even more to fans, causing him to become an even bigger star without the mask.

Over the next year, things became tense in the EMLL offices, as Antonio Peña was having difficulties with other office staff and Paco Alonso. Despite the record-setting box office success taking place at Arena México that was due to a three-way feud with Konnan battling Perro Aguayo and Cien Caras, Konnan was feeling resentment from many of the locker room veterans who also held positions in EMLL's front office.

During this time, Konnan was also brought into Vince McMahon's World Wrestling Federation. They had collaborated on a character called Max Moon. The original idea was for Konnan to enter the ring with an elaborate robot costume that would shoot explosions out of the arms. After several months of working with the promotion, which correlated with his success in Mexico, he decided to focus on lucha libre over the WWF.

Antonio Peña and Konnan began to secretly make plans to break out on their own. Peña was the one who had connections with Televisa, and he was able to negotiate a deal to have them back a new promotion. On May 7, 1992, Peña and Konnan, along with over twenty wrestlers, appeared at a hotel next to the Televisa main office for a press conference. It was there that they announced the formation of a new promotion, Asistencia Asesoría y Administración (AAA). One week later, AAA held its first event in Veracruz, and a week after that, Konnan debuted with AAA at a television taping in Léon, Guanajuato.

To say that AAA was a success right out of the gate would be shortsighted. It was a huge success immediately. Even while having trouble locking down a regular building in the Distrito Federal, the company toured across Mexico, packing buildings at every turn. In less than a year's time, AAA made plans to present an annual event called Triplemanía.

The first Triplemanía would be held at the forty-two thousand-seat bullring Plaza de México. The main event selected for the evening would be Konnan battling rival Cien Caras, and to add to the importance of the match, it was declared the loser of the match would retire. On April 30, 1993, in front of a record crowd for lucha libre of nearly fifty thousand fans, Konnan lost that match to his rival Cien Caras. Due to the controversial ending, which saw WWF wrestler Jake "The Snake" Roberts distract Konnan, a letter-writing campaign began in Mexico to allow Konnan to return.

While out of the ring in Mexico, he continued to wrestle in the US as AAA was making headway in California. On August 28, 1993, Konnan faced Cien Caras and Jake "the Snake" Roberts, the man guilty of forcing him to lose the retirement match, in a triangle match. Anticipation was so high that they sold out the Los Angeles Sports Arena and turned away an estimated eight thousand fans, causing huge traffic jams all around the arena. The match drew the largest crowd for wrestling in the US for that year, beating even WWF numbers.

Over the following years, after a combination of the devaluing of the peso and interest from promoters in the US, Konnan began making appearances for Extreme Championship Wrestling (ECW), based in Philadelphia, Pennsylvania. His short but memorable stint with the company led to Konnan being offered a position with Ted Turner's World Championship Wrestling (WCW). Konnan was now working for WCW, the company that was battling WWF neck and neck as the number one wrestling company in the world.

Fans of wrestling's "attitude era" will remember Konnan coming to the ring, grabbing the microphone, and yelling, *"Orale! Arriba la Raza!"* to packed arenas as part of WCW's New World Order faction. After WCW, Konnan would go on to be featured in TNA/IMPACT Wrestling as the company sought to compete with the WWE and star in season one of the *Lucha Underground* TV series from filmmaker Robert Rodriguez and

Mark Burnett. Since 2018, Konnan has also been working as a writer and producer for Lucha Libre AAA, where he has a recurring on-camera role as a villainous foil to the *técnicos* (good guys) of the company.

Along with his legendary career inside the ring, Konnan will also be most remembered for being an ambassador of lucha libre in the US and around the world. He has championed the careers of up-and-coming luchadores to gain greater exposure and can be credited with introducing such stars as Rey Mysterio, Juventud Guerrera, and Psychosis to American fans. At one time, Konnan was the biggest box office attraction in Mexico; however, his legacy might be remembered best as the man who introduced modern lucha libre to the masses of American pop culture by convincing promoters to take a chance on the style.

CALDO DE RES
(TRADITIONAL MEXICAN BEEF SOUP)

SERVES
4

SOUP:

3 pounds (1.4 kg) beef oxtail, short ribs, shanks, or beef cubes

Kosher salt

2 ears corn, cut into quarters

2 large Yukon Gold potatoes, peeled and diced into ¼-inch (6 mm) cubes

2 medium-size carrots, peeled and diced into ¼-inch (6 mm) cubes

1 handful of fresh cilantro, chopped

MEXICAN RICE:

1 tablespoon (15 ml) olive oil

2 garlic cloves, finely chopped

½ medium-size red onion, finely chopped

1 cup (195 g) uncooked long-grain rice

2 cups (475 ml) beef stock

½ cup (123 g) tomato sauce

Kosher salt

3 cilantro sprigs, finely chopped

RECIPE CONTINUED >

Talk about keeping it in the lucha family—this recipe is the result of marriage, friendship, and some multicultural adaptation.

Konnan is a hugely important figure in the modern lucha libre world, but he was also pivotal in guiding Rey Mysterio in becoming one of the most popular luchadores out there, too. Not only are these two legends close, but so are their wives—they even swap recipes! This recipe comes from Konnan's wife, Stacey, a native Australian who was schooled in how to make Caldo de Res by Rey Mysterio's wife, Angelika.

Made using slow-cooked beef, a hearty serving of vegetables, and served with Mexican rice and tortillas, this is a warming dish that's perfect for sharing with friends.

1. Make the soup: Fill a 6-quart pot with 4½ quarts (4.25 L) of water over high heat. Add the beef oxtail and salt to taste. Bring to a boil. Once boiling, remove the film of fat that forms at the top. Lower the heat to medium and cook for about 1½ hours, removing additional film from the top as needed.

2. Add the quartered ears of corn; continue to cook for 30 minutes.

TO SERVE (QUANTITIES TO TASTE):

Corn or flour tortillas, warmed

Lime wedges

Salsa picante (hot sauce)

Serving Suggestion

For the hot sauce, Stacey recommends using Valentina, but Tapitío or any hot sauce will work well.

3. Add the potatoes, carrots, and cilantro. Continue to cook for an additional 30 minutes, or until all the ingredients are softened and fully cooked and the beef is falling off the bone. Add salt to taste.

4. Make the rice: Heat the olive oil in a medium-size saucepan over medium heat. Once hot, stir in the garlic and onion; cook for 2 to 3 minutes, or until softened and golden brown.

5. Add the rice and stir for 2 to 3 minutes, until golden brown.

6. Add the beef stock and tomato sauce. Bring the mixture to a boil. Once boiling, lower the heat to a simmer and cook for 20 to 25 minutes, or until the rice is cooked and has absorbed the liquid. Add salt to taste and garnish with the cilantro.

7. To serve, divide the soup among bowls, add the Mexican rice, and serve with warm tortillas, lime wedges, and salsa picante on the side.

CARNE ASADA MARINADE

ENOUGH FOR
3 lbs
of steak

1 (12-ounce [355 ml]) bottle
Modelo Negro beer

½ cup (170 g) honey

½ medium-size yellow onion

4 garlic cloves, crushed

1 jalapeño pepper

2 tablespoons (22 g) Dijon mustard

1 tablespoon (15 ml) Tabasco sauce

1 teaspoon (5 ml) Worcestershire
sauce

Juice of 2 limes

½ teaspoon (3 g) kosher salt

½ teaspoon (1 g) freshly ground
black pepper

3 pounds (1.4 kg) flank steak

No self-respecting luchador is without a great carne asada recipe, but although meat matters, the real magic is in the marinade. This recipe from luchadora Taya Valkyrie is bound to become your brand-new favorite.

It's sweet, savory, sour, citrusy, and has a little umami too. It's the perfect tenderizer (and flavorizer) for your favorite steak. There's only one way to make it better: add a heaping side of Loca Guacamole (page 22) and some veggies on the side (Taya likes grilled green bell peppers and corn on the cob) to make it a meal.

1. In a blender, combine all the ingredients, except the steak. Blend until smooth.
2. Put the steak in a large resealable plastic freezer bag. Add the marinade. Seal and refrigerate for 2 hours, or overnight.
3. Remove the steak from the marinade (discard the marinade). Grill the steak on medium-high heat for 4 minutes on each side until it's medium well done and has an internal temperature of 165°F (73°C). Set aside for 3 minutes to cool. Cut as desired.

See pages 18–22 for Taya Valkyrie's story and Loca Guacamole recipe.

THE REAL MAGIC *is in the marinade*

STEP ONE COMBINE INGREDIENTS.

JERRY VILLAGRANA

 FROM **EL PASO, TX**

JERRY VILLAGRANA GREW up in El Paso, Texas, and first attended a lucha libre show across the border in Juárez, Mexico, before he was two years old. He was instantly hooked and it became his greatest childhood passion. At that time, Eddie Guerrero was the hometown legend and would often face Konnan, Ari Romero, and even take the hair of Negro Casas after a classic Hair vs. Hair apuesta match. Young Jerry became passionate about collecting masks, figures, and lucha libre magazines.

While Spanish was spoken in the Villagrana household, growing up in the US, he learned how to read English in school. But with lucha magazines in hand, he would soon teach himself how to read Spanish. He knew the luchadores' names by heart, and in no time at all, he was able to develop his Spanish reading fluency to match his verbal fluency.

After graduating as a mechanical engineer from the University of Texas at El Paso, Villagrana went to work for General Motors in Detroit. Jerry would also become an event photographer and began shooting independent wrestling events in 2013. A work assignment would send Jerry; his wife, Robyn; and their children to Mexico in 2015. Having contributed photos to the legendary *Pro Wrestling Illustrated* magazine in the past, and now living in Mexico, Jerry had the honor of covering the 2015 Lucha Libre World Cup event from Lucha Libre AAA for the magazine. AAA liked his work so much that it invited him to shoot its next major event, Verano de Escándalo, as a ringside photographer. He then received an invitation to shoot the biggest event in all of lucha libre each year, AAA's Triplemanía. But it wasn't just the big leagues Jerry covered.

During his time in Mexico, from 2015 to 2018, he would cover dozens of independent events in Northern Mexico. His work and unique style caught the eye of Masked Republic, and Jerry's work was heavily featured on the company's new LuchaCentral.com website. Back in the US, Jerry continues to shoot events, including WWE,

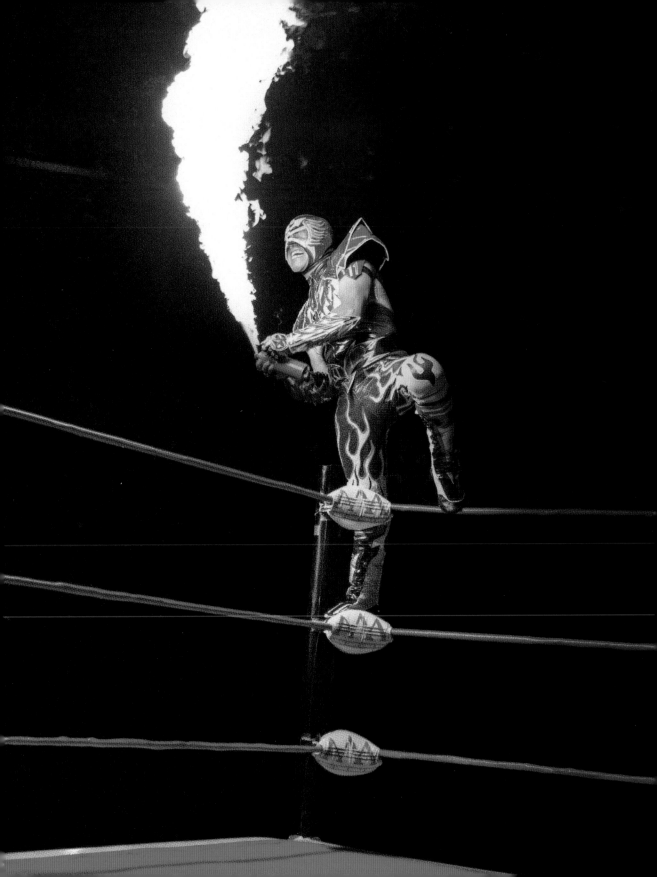

IMPACT Wrestling, and Ring of Honor shows, but his passion for lucha libre still burns bright.

Jerry also has passed his passion for lucha libre down to his children, who can be seen at times in promotional photos for Masked Republic products, including the company's officially licensed costumes.

"We moved to Mexico when my son was two years old, which was the same age I was when I got my first lucha mask and fell in love with the sport," Jerry said. "For him, luchadores are basically superheroes, except you can actually meet them and see them live in action. My daughter won't tell you that she loves lucha, but at shows she is often the loudest voice in the crowd! Even my wife appreciates the athleticism in the action, the culture in the costumes, and the family friendly nature of it."

CARNE ASADA STREET TACOS

SERVES
6 to 8

3 pounds (1.4 kg) flank steak

1 (12-ounce [355 ml]) can lager beer

Juice of 2 oranges

1 bunch cilantro separated into stalks and leaves

4 garlic cloves, smashed

2 teaspoons (5 g) ground cumin

2 tablespoons (30 ml) vegetable oil

Salt and freshly ground black pepper

TO SERVE:

6 to 8 small corn tortillas

Chopped raw onion

Tomatillo Salsa or Garden Salsa (recipes follow), enough for 6 to 8 tortillas

Lime wedges

Taco 'bout a fantastic recipe—these carne asada street tacos come from well-known lucha photographer Jerry Villagrana, who learned the art of grilling from his father.

According to Villagrana, his father didn't drink beer very often, but there was always one on hand for the days when he made carne asada. He had a whole weekend routine: marinate the meat, then grill the carne asada just in time for CMLL and AAA broadcasts!

Why not follow the Villagrana family lead? Enjoy these tacos with a beer and some lucha libre on TV and let the good times roll!

NOTE: When grilling meat, you should never poke it, and make sure to let it cool a bit after it's off the grill. Following these tips will help you minimize any of the moisture escaping.

1. Place the steak, beer, orange juice, cilantro stalks, garlic, cumin, vegetable oil, and a little salt and pepper in a large bowl and use your hands to mix them all together.

2. Cover the bowl and let marinate for at least 1 hour in the refrigerator but no more than 4 hours.

3. Remove the steak and discard the marinade. On an outdoor grill or in a saucepan over high heat on the stovetop, grill the steak to your desired level of doneness.

4. Remove from the heat and let cool for at least 5 minutes to keep the juices sealed in the meat.

5. Cut the cooked steak across the grain into strips about the width of a finger.

6. On a griddle over medium-low heat, warm the tortillas and place them in a folded kitchen towel to keep warm.

7. To serve, place portions of steak on warm tortillas and top with onion, cilantro leaves, and salsa to taste. Serve with lime wedges on the side.

TOMATILLO SALSA
Makes 3 to 4 cups (780 ml to 1 L) salsa

8 tomatillos

2 large green tomatoes (unripe)

10 fresh serrano peppers

Kosher salt

1. Preheat the oven to 400°F (200°C).

2. On a baking sheet, arrange the tomatillos, tomatoes, and peppers in a single layer. Alternatively, preheat an outdoor grill to high and place the tomatillos, tomatoes, and peppers on the grill.

3. Bake (or grill), rotating as needed until all sides of tomatoes and peppers are charred, in 6 to 9 minutes.

4. Mash in a molcajete (mortar and pestle) or blend in a blender; add salt to taste.

GARDEN SALSA
Makes 3 to 4 cups (780 ml to 1 L) salsa

4 poblano peppers

6 to 8 jalapeño peppers

8 Roma tomatoes

Kosher salt

1. Preheat the oven to 400°F (200°C).

2. On a baking sheet, arrange the peppers and tomatoes in a single layer. Alternatively, preheat an outside grill to high and place the peppers and tomatoes on the grill.

3. Bake (or grill), rotating as needed until all sides of tomatoes and peppers are charred, in 6 to 9 minutes.

4. Mash in a molcajete (mortar and pestle) or blend in a blender; add salt to taste.

See page 204 for Jerry Villagrana's Pollo Asado.

CHICKEN CHORIZO CHIMICHANGAS

MAKES
20
chimichangas

2½ cups (590 ml) corn oil

9 ounces (255 g) soy chorizo

3 pounds (1.4 kg) chicken, cut into chunks

20 egg roll wrappers

1 large egg, lightly beaten

Sylvia Romo Muñoz, co-owner of SBWA and talented home chef, has a definite devilish streak. This guilty pleasure recipe comes from her alter ego Luchafer luchadora Alacrana Plata. This lively luchadora understands that sometimes you just need something fatty, satisfying, and a little naughty. These chicken chorizo chimichangas check all the right boxes.

Unlike traditional chimichangas, this recipe uses egg roll wrappers instead of tortillas and the filling includes a unique mix of chicken and soy chorizo. Not quite the textbook version but tremendously satisfying—especially when served with a side of homemade creamy guacamole.

NOTE: Not feeling the soy joy? Traditional chorizo can also be used in this recipe.

1. In a large saucepan, combine 1 tablespoon (15 ml) of the corn oil and the chorizo. Cook the chorizo for 2 to 3 minutes over medium heat.
2. Add the chicken; stir to combine. Cook for 10 to 15 minutes, or until the chicken is thoroughly cooked and has reached an internal temperature of 165°F (73°C). Remove from the heat and let cool briefly.
3. Shred the chicken.
4. In a second large saucepan, heat the remaining oil until it reaches a frying temperature of 350°F to 375°F (180° to 190°C).

5. Assemble your chimichangas: Place an egg roll wrapper with a corner facing you. Spread a generous spoonful of the chicken mixture across the surface of the wrapper, leaving a small portion uncovered along the edges. Roll from the corner facing you, folding in the sides as you roll to create a seal. Use the beaten egg mixture to seal the wrapper (this will ensure it won't pop open during frying). Repeat with the remaining wrappers and chicken mixture.

6. Place about five chimichangas in the hot oil, about ½ inch (1.3 cm) apart. Cook for about 5 minutes, or until browned on the first side; flip and repeat cooking for another 5 minutes on the second side. Once golden brown and crispy, remove from the hot oil using tongs. Blot any excess oil on paper towels. Repeat with the remaining chimichangas. Serve with guacamole (recipe follows).

GUACAMOLE
Makes 2½ cups (563 g) guacamole

3 large ripe avocados, peeled, pitted, and mashed

1½ teaspoons (7.5 ml) freshly squeezed lime juice

3 tablespoons (49 g) salsa

1 tablespoon (14 g) mayonnaise

1 tablespoon (15 g) sour cream

½ teaspoon (3 g) kosher salt

½ teaspoon (1 g) freshly ground black pepper

½ teaspoon (1.3 g) ground cumin

¼ teaspoon (0.8 g) garlic powder

1. In a large bowl, mix together all the ingredients until blended.

2. Cover and refrigerate for 1 to 2 hours before serving.

See pages 32–35 for Sylvia Muñoz's story and Spanish Rice, and page 291 for her Skinny Tequila Sunrise.

LIZ FAIRBAIRN

 **SANTA CRUZ, CA**

THE WORLD OF Lucha VaVOOM is an amazing mix of lucha libre, burlesque, and performance art that plays in front of sold-out crowds in Hollywood and special performances around the globe. It's a wild mash-up brought to life by Liz Fairbairn and her business partner, Rita D'Albert. Liz was introduced to lucha libre while working on location in Mexico for her career in television. Liz was already a fan of Rita's work producing a burlesque revival show, *The Velvet Hammer Burlesque*, and finally convinced Rita to attend an event. It's a good thing she did because Rita fell in love with lucha the moment she witnessed her first show at the Grand Olympic Auditorium. And with that, the two came together to create this amazing take of a live lucha libre experience.

Often, VaVOOM events have special themes that will intertwine story lines throughout the show. They are also produced so that new fans who attend will easily be able to follow along. Another aspect unique to Lucha VaVOOM are the comedian commentators who narrate what you are watching live. The list of names who have lent their talents to the commentary table is impressive, with such stars as Fred Armisen, Blaine Capatch, Patton Oswalt, Ron Funches, Chris Hardwick, Dana Gould, Tom Kenny, and Jeff Davis.

Along with famous comedians behind the mic, it is not uncommon to see celebrities sitting ringside, enjoying the show. Not only have Drew Carey, Paul Reubens (Pee-Wee Herman), David Arquette, and the late Robin Williams been spotted ringside during the matches, but the company has had its fair share of famous luchadores perform at its events. Some of Mexico's biggest stars, including El Hijo del Santo, LA Park, Blue Demon Jr., Dr. Wagner Jr., Los Brazos, Los Villanos, and Mil Máscaras, have appeared.

Lucha VaVOOM is an experience that is difficult to describe with only written words. Even photos do not really do the live experience justice, but they do give a glimpse into the vibrant world that is uniquely theirs.

CHICKEN ENCHILADAS SUIZAS

SERVES
4

2¼ cups (532 ml) vegetable oil or (468 g) manteca (lard)

1½ pounds (680 g) boneless, skinless chicken thighs, cut into 1½-inch (4 cm) cubes

10 to 12 tomatillos, chopped into ½-inch (1.3 cm) cubes

1 large white onion, chopped into ½-inch (1.3 cm) cubes (about 1½ cups [240 g])

2 to 4 garlic cloves, finely chopped

1 to 2 jalapeño peppers, finely chopped

1 (24-ounce [680 g]) jar chunky green salsa or salsa verde

(Fairbairn prefers Herdez brand but says any chunky salsa verde is fine. Often she will use La Victoria, which is widely available. She recommends one without vinegar, if possible.)

RECIPE CONTINUED >

Pleasuretown population: YOU. These *enchiladas suizas* start with rich, aromatic chicken and vegetables combined with plenty of cheese, which are then wrapped in cream-coated tortillas and coated with even more cheese. Then, you cook them to crispy, golden, bubbling cheesy perfection. In case you didn't get it: cheese!

Yup, this may just be the ultimate comfort food casserole. Best of all, it's perfect for a crowd; according to Liz Fairbairn, founder and owner of Lucha VaVOOM, "I also usually cook for an army." The leftovers taste great too.

1. Preheat the oven to 350°F (180°C).
2. In a large saucepan over medium heat, heat ¼ cup (60 ml) of the vegetable oil (or 52 g of the lard). Once hot, add the chicken. Let it brown on both sides for about 3 minutes, but don't cook fully.
3. Add the tomatillos, onion, garlic, and jalapeños to the pan with the chicken. Sauté the vegetables until tender, about 5 minutes. You can add a bit of water to reduce while cooking.
4. Add the salsa and chicken stock.
5. Simmer the filling until it's a thick liquid, about 5 minutes; add more jalapeños if you prefer a spicier dish, and salt and pepper to taste as it cooks.
6. Prepare your workstation: Pour the cream in a shallow pan and set aside (you'll use this later for dipping the fried tortillas). Have

1 cup (240 ml) chicken stock

Salt and freshly ground black pepper

2 cups (475 ml) heavy cream

30 large, soft white corn tortillas

1 pound (455 g) shredded Monterey
Jack or similar mild white cheese

ready an 11 x 15-inch (28 x 38 cm) Pyrex or metal casserole dish for the finished enchiladas.

7. In a large, deep saucepan, heat the remaining 2 cups (472 ml) of oil (or 416 g lard) for frying the tortillas.

8. Lightly fry the tortillas in the hot oil for 30 to 60 seconds, or until golden brown but not crispy (usually when the tortilla bubbles in the center it is ready to be transferred), then transfer carefully to the pan of cream.

9. Allow the tortillas to soften in the cream, flipping to cover both sides, then transfer to the baking dish.

10. As you transfer each tortilla, spoon about ¼ cup (75 g) of the chicken chile verde on top and add a handful of shredded cheese (reserve some cheese for sprinkling on the top of the casserole). Roll the tortilla carefully, and folded side down, align each enchilada in the baking pan. Don't be afraid to nestle them closely! It will keep them from unraveling.

11. When the baking dish is full, pour some of the remaining cream (not too much) over the enchiladas, and add the remaining salsa from the pan. Sprinkle the remaining shredded cheese on top. Bake until bubbly and golden on top.

THE LUCHA BROTHERS

(Penta Zero M and Rey Fenix)

 MEXICO CITY, MEXICO • **DECEMBER 2015 (AS A TEAM)**

IN MANY WAYS, you could say lucha libre is a family business, mainly because almost every single luchador ever was the son, daughter, brother, sister, cousin, nephew, or niece of a luchador. It's the sort of thing that's led to the creation of so-called dynasties, such as the Casas Family, the Alvarado/Brazo Family, the Tapia Family, and on and on. All this to say that it should come as no surprise that two luchadores would eventually come along and form a tag team that was called the Lucha Brothers. It just so happened to be Penta Zero M (also known as Pentagón Jr.) and Rey Fenix, arguably the two most popular luchadores in Mexico and the United States today.

Their brotherly bond related to lucha libre did not start in the ring though. While growing up, the future Penta and Fenix would sell masks to fans and passersby in front of the historic Arena México, dreaming of the day that they would be able to actually become luchadores themselves. But even in their wildest dreams, they did not think that in the next ten years, they would become the most popular luchadores on the entire planet, having their masks sold, not only in arenas in Mexico, but costume shops across the US. Their merchandise even stretches into categories most other luchadores have only dreamed of, including action figures, comic books, and a forthcoming pinball machine.

And yet, like most brothers, they started out going against each other. Born in Mexico City to luchador Fuego (not to be confused with the luchador by the same name who was on TV for CMLL), Penta and Fenix got into the wrestling business together, but not as partners. Instead, Pentagón Jr. started out as Zarius and eventually was named Dark Dragón before taking on the Pentagón Jr. persona in order to feud with the first Octagón Jr., while Fenix started out as

Máscara Oriental. Nevertheless, the two were always around each other and even managed to tangle in the ring a few times between Lucha Libre AAA, *Lucha Underground* (where they both became stars), and even US indie powerhouse Pro Wrestling Guerrilla (PWG). It was at PWG in Los Angeles where the two finally formed a full-time team in 2016.

Since then, the Lucha Brothers have transitioned from great singles stars into great tag stars who can also be singles stars. Together they have conquered every promotion they've stepped into, from AAA, Consejo Mundial de Lucha Libre, and The Crash in Mexico to DEFY, AAW, IMPACT Wrestling, Major League Wrestling, and now All Elite Wrestling in the United States. In the process, they've also managed to win some awards.

As of this writing, the duo have had ten Tag Team Championship reigns among nine different promotions, including two reigns as the AAA World Tag Team Champions in Mexico. They have been voted Tag Team of the Year by CBS Sports and voted Tag Team of the Year twice by the readers of the premier lucha libre news site LuchaCentral.com. In 2019, the brothers joined US-based wrestling league All Elite Wrestling, where they are always attempting to be champions and prove they are the "best tag team in the universe." Who could argue this point when you have a guy who can fly like Fenix (named "Most Spectacular Luchador" two years in a row by LuchaCentral.com readers) and a luchador who pummels like Penta teaming together? And they're brothers!

PENTA ZERO M

FROM **MEXICO CITY, MEXICO** ✦ DEBUT **APRIL 2007**

HE WAS ORIGINALLY created as the foil for the first of several luchadores named Octagón Jr. Instead of ending up as the foil to a bigger star, Penta Zero M has since become one of the most recognizable luchadores in both Mexico and around the globe, where he's an almost cultlike hero. With a look best described as "zombie ninja skeleton," an arm-breaking ruthless streak, and an all-time great catchphrase ("*Cero Miedo*" ["Zero fear"]), Penta has become a top singles and tag star wherever he's gone, most notably winning the world championships in both *Lucha Underground* and IMPACT Wrestling. These days, he's wreaking havoc in All Elite Wrestling and Lucha Libre AAA, teaming with his brother Rey Fenix to form the Lucha Brothers, arguably the best tag team in all of wrestling.

FUN FACTS

★ Penta Zero M first competed in Lucha Libre AAA under the name Dark Dragón.

★ He also goes by the names Pentagón Jr., Penta El Zero M, and even Penta 0M.

★ He's the favorite wrestler of San Francisco 49ers star George Kittle, who has adopted Penta's "Cero Miedo" catchphrase and taunt, which he does on the field after every first down.

CHICKEN FAJITAS WITH BELL PEPPERS

SERVES
4

1 boneless, skinless chicken breast, cut into ½-inch (1.3 cm)-thick strips

2 red bell peppers, seeded and julienned

2 green bell peppers, seeded and julienned

1 medium-size white onion, julienned

Juice of 3 limes

3 tablespoons (45 ml) Maggi Jugo seasoning sauce

3 tablespoons (45 ml) Worcestershire sauce

Salt and freshly ground black pepper

3 tablespoons (45 ml) extra-virgin olive oil

4 medium tortillas, per serving

Fajitas are a Mexican classic. That means for any self-respecting Mexican, there's a ton of pressure to have a great and reliable recipe that works every time. Luckily, Penta Zero M is a luchador who fights and lives with "*cero miedo*"—zero fear!—and offers up a recipe that you can approach fearlessly in the kitchen.

You can't go wrong with this recipe, which comes together quickly and easily, and yields highly satisfying results. Feel like burrito-izing it? Substitute this fajita chicken for the regular chicken called for in his brother Rey Fenix's burrito recipe (page 176), for a Lucha Brothers Burrito Especial!

1. In a large bowl, combine the chicken strips, bell peppers, onion, lime juice, Maggi seasoning sauce, Worcestershire sauce, and salt and black pepper. Let marinate in the refrigerator for about 30 minutes.
2. In a saucepan, heat the olive oil in a large pot over medium heat. Transfer the chicken, onion, and peppers to the pan (discard the marinade) and cook for 5 to 8 minutes, or until softened. Add salt and pepper to taste.
3. Serve with warm tortillas on the side.

See pages 174–178 for Rey Fenix's story and MexaKing Wrap.

LADY APACHE

FROM **MEXICO CITY, MEXICO** • DEBUT **JUNE 1986**

SANDRA GONZÁLEZ CALDERÓN may be the world's most dangerous grandmother, who just happens to be a luchadora. Sandra was born June 26, 1970, in Mexico City, but her alter ego Lady Apache was born on the mat in a ring in 1986.

At a young age, Sandra married Mario Balbuena González, a luchador who wrestled under the name Gran Apache. (Mario has become one of lucha libre's most respected trainers and he was one of the trainers responsible for teaching his then wife the skills to become a luchadora.) When she debuted, opportunities for women in lucha libre were very limited, so she spent some of her time taking bookings as a valet for Gran Apache and his partner to form a team called Los Gran Apaches. They were working for a promotion based out of the Pavillón Azteca and had a television show called *Super Lunes*. The company was geared toward children and garnered high ratings on television during the 1980s.

During her first marriage, to Gran Apache, Sandra became stepmother to two women who also went on to become luchadores, Faby Apache and Mari Apache. Her marriage to Gran Apache lasted only a few years and she soon moved to CMLL, where she began dating and eventually married Jésus Alvarado Nieves, aka Brazo de Oro, of the Alvarado family. Brazo de Oro was part of Los Brazos, one of lucha libre's top trios during the '80s and '90s.

Lady Apache married into one of Mexico's largest lucha libre families when she wed Brazo de Oro, son of the family patriarch, Juan Alvarado Ibarra, who wrestled under the name Shadito ("Little Shadow") Cruz, due to his similar appearance to the legendary Black Shadow. Shadito had six sons, all of whom took to lucha libre and all of whom had children that went into lucha libre. Some of the members of the Alvarado family include La Máscara, Psycho Clown, Robin, Máximo, El Brazo Jr., Goya Kong, Carta Brava Jr., and India Sioux.

Apache's new family was not only one of lucha's largest wrestling families, but they also carried a lot of political power as well. Brazo de Oro was head of the wrestler's union and worked in the offices of CMLL. During her time working with CMLL, Lady Apache became a three-time CMLL World Women's Champion and a two-time Mexican National Women's Champion.

Her first World Championship came on November 8, 1996, when she competed in a four-woman tournament to crown a new champion. After defeating her first-round opponent, Xóchitl Hamada, she went on to the finals later that evening and pinned Chaparrita Asari to win the World Championship at the cathedral of lucha libre, Arena México.

Sometime later, she moved on from CMLL and her marriage to Brazo de Oro and found herself wrestling for Asistencia Asesoría y Administración, AAA. There, she married her current husband, Edgar Luna Pozos, who wrestles as Electroshock. Her lucha family grew with her marriage to Edgar. Edgar's brother Jesús competes under the name Charly Manson or a variety of aliases, including Charlie Malice, Sharlie Rockstar, and Charly Rockstar.

While in AAA, she teamed with her husband to compete in mixed tag team matches. On June 15, 2003, at AAA's Triplemanía XI, Lady Apache and Electroshock defeated the teams of Martha Vilalobos and former brother-in-law El Brazo, Tiffany and Chessman, and ex-husband Gran Apache and step-daughter Faby Apache. The team became the first AAA World Mixed Tag Team Champion in front of a huge crowd at El Toreo de Cuatro Caminos in Naucalpan. (This may also potentially have been the first lucha libre match featuring a luchadora and TWO ex-husbands!)

Lady Apache twice won the prestigious AAA Reina de Reinas championship, once on February 17, 2001, and then on February 1, 2004. A month later, at the Rey de Reyes event, Apache teamed with her husband, Electroshock, in a *parejas suicida* match where the losing team would be forced to wrestle each other in a luchas de apuestas match. They were beaten by their opponents, Chessman and Tiffany, when Chessman pinned Lady Apache, forcing husband and wife to wrestle. When Electroshock pinned his wife, he pleaded to allow his own head to get shaved instead of having Apache lose her hair!

Over the following decade she wrestled all over North America and Japan, capturing championships and competing with the best in the world. She would move back and forth from AAA to CMLL as well as smaller promotions in Mexico and took numerous tours to top women promotions in Japan. She has won the most prestigious women's lucha libre championship in the US, Pro Wrestling Revolution Women's World Championship, on three occasions and has defended the title in both Mexico and Japan.

Lady Apache is part of some of lucha libre's largest legacies and has earned the respect of her peers as one of the best luchadoras of all time.

CHILES EN NOGADA

SERVES
8

NOGADA SAUCE:

1 cup (100 g) walnuts

2 cups (475 ml) whole milk

1½ cups (345 g) sour cream

¼ pound (about 115 g) queso
fresco (aka queso blanco)

1½ tablespoons (19 g) sugar

¼ teaspoon (0.6 g) ground
cinnamon

½ teaspoon (3 g) kosher salt

STUFFED PEPPERS:

8 poblano peppers

2 tablespoons (30 ml) extra-virgin
olive oil

1 tablespoon (14 g) unsalted butter
at room temperature

½ medium-size white onion, diced

1 pound (455 g) ground turkey

1 (14.5-ounce [441 g]) can crushed
roasted tomato

1 apple, cored and cut into quarters

½ cup (75 g) golden raisins

2 tablespoons (18 g) sliced almonds

RECIPE CONTINUED >

Chiles en nogada is kind of like the fancier and more cosmopolitan cousin of another classic Mexican dish, *chiles rellenos*. Both dishes start with poblano peppers stuffed with a flavorful meat mixture, but the nogada version features a generous blanket of walnut-cream sauce and jewel-like pomegranate seeds on top.

Lady Apache's recipe is a tour de force: smoky, flame-cooked peppers are stuffed with an aromatic meat mixture and topped with a crave-worthy cream sauce garnished with parsley and pomegranate seeds to resemble the Mexican flag. Although this dish is typically served around Mexico's Independence Day in September, it's a delight year-round. See for yourself why it's such a classic.

1. Make the sauce: Combine the nuts and milk in a large bowl. Cover and place in the refrigerator for least 2 hours or as long as overnight. This step will take away any bitter flavor in the nuts.

2. Drain the walnuts; transfer to a blender. Add the sour cream, cheese, sugar, cinnamon, and salt. Blend briefly on low speed to incorporate; increase the speed to high and blend for about 1 minute, or until smooth and creamy in texture. Set aside.

3. Make the stuffed peppers: Grill the poblano peppers over a stovetop flame, placing each one directly on the fire for 2 to 3 minutes, turning frequently, and allowing the skin to blacken and bubble on all sides. You can also do this with a grill pan, but it will take at least double the amount of time.

¾ teaspoon (1.8 g) ground cinnamon

1 teaspoon (6 g) kosher salt

½ teaspoon (1 g) ground black pepper

Pinch of ground cloves

1½ cups (338 g) pomegranate seeds

¼ cup (15 g) fresh parsley, finely chopped

4. Once roasted, place the grilled peppers in a bowl and cover with plastic wrap. Let rest, covered, for about 15 minutes. This will help them release steam, making them easier to peel.

5. Use a damp towel to help you peel the peppers. Once unpeeled, remove the centers and seeds, reserving the seeds for later use.

6. In a large skillet, heat the oil and butter over medium heat. Once the butter has melted, add the onion. Cook for 3 to 4 minutes, or until transparent.

7. Add the ground turkey. Cook for 8 to 10 minutes, or until completely browned. Add the tomato, apple, raisins, almonds, and spices. If you like your stuffed peppers spicy, add the reserved poblano seeds. Lower the heat and simmer for 5 to 6 minutes to allow the flavors to combine.

8. To serve, make a 2- to 3-inch (5 to 7.5 cm) cut lengthwise in each grilled pepper. Evenly divide the meat mixture among the peppers and top with nogada sauce. To garnish, sprinkle a stripe of finely chopped parsley on top of the peppers near the stem; leave a portion in the middle white, then add a stripe of pomegranate seeds.

MASCARITA DORADA

 VERACRUZ, MEXICO ◆ **JANUARY 2000**

AS PART OF lucha libre's Mini-Estrella division (short wrestler, many of whom have dwarfism), Mascarita Dorada is one of Mexico's most respected "minis"! He began his career by being handed a name that carried a lot of history with it. With very little experience, he was given the name Mascarita Sagrada (often referred to as Mascarita Sagrada 2000) on his debut with AAA. Prior to his wearing the mask, two others before him wore the same mask. The first Mascarita Sagrada was famous for his runs in CMLL, then AAA, and was wrestling for both WCW and WWF during the Monday Night Wars as Mascarita Sagrada and Mini Nova. He was followed by Mascarita Sagrada Jr., who also went on to work for the WWF but was repackaged as Max Mini.

Although he was unrecognizable due to the furry costume he wore in the film, while working in AAA as Mascarita Sagrada, he also played the very memorable role of El Lobo #2 in the most famous lucha libre comedy of all time, *Nacho Libre*.

In 2007, he left AAA to join rival promotion CMLL, where he changed his name to Mascarita Dorada and found great success. In 2008, with CMLL, he won its Pequeño Reyes del Aire tournament. In fact, his popularity grew so large that for the first time in the history of lucha libre, a "full-size" luchador was created based on a mini rather than the traditional manner of a mini's character being based on a typical-size luchador. Mascarita Dorada became a huge sensation in his own right as well. After some time, Mascarita moved away from CMLL to compete independently before returning to AAA for a few years.

In 2013 he signed with World Wrestling Entertainment, where he was given the name El Torito as a mascot for Los Matadores. While working with WWE, he was able to compete in matches such as the 2014 Royal Rumble and the first *ever* WeeLC Match.

The WeeLC Match led to a lucha de apuestas Mask vs. Hair match at WWE's Payback pay-per-view. It was there where he faced and defeated Hornswoggle for his hair in one of the highest-profile matches of his career. Apuestas matches are extremely rare outside Mexico, especially in the biggest wrestling company in the world, WWE.

Not long after, Mascarita Dorada left WWE and returned to his former name and got right back to being considered the best mini luchador in all of Mexico. He also appeared on the TV series *Lucha Underground* in a number of roles, including Mascarita Sagrada 2000 and El Bunny. The mini of many masks has also worked on and off for Lucha VaVOOM in roles including El Lobo and Lil' Chicken.

Mascarita Dorada continues to appear at lucha libre events around the world and will definitely be etched into the lucha libre history books as one of the greatest Mini-Estrellas of all time.

CHIMICHURRI TUNA FILLET

SERVES
2

½ cup (120 ml) extra-virgin
  olive oil

2 tablespoons (19 g) finely chopped
  garlic

¼ cup (15 g) fresh parsley, finely
  chopped

¼ cup (10 g) fresh cilantro, finely
  chopped, plus more to taste

2 tablespoons (28 g) salted butter

2 (4-ounce [115 g]) portions fresh
  tuna

Kosher salt

8 asparagus stalks

1 (4-inch [10 cm] slice French bread

Be warned: Chimichurri—a green sauce with dominant flavors of olive oil, garlic, cilantro, and parsley—is an addictive substance. It's one of those magical sauces that, once you try it, you'll want to put it on everything from eggs to pizza to meat. It's only fitting that its zippy taste is a favorite of one of the zippiest and most amazingly acrobatic mini luchadores in the history of the sport—Mascarita Dorada.

In this recipe, the chimichurri adds an elegant visual appeal and a highly pleasing flavor to seared tuna. Served alongside grilled asparagus and crusty French bread, this is restaurant-caliber fare that you can enjoy at home, perfect for celebrating your favorite luchador's next win.

1. Make the chimichurri: Heat the olive oil in a medium-size saucepan over medium heat. Once hot, add the garlic, parsley, and cilantro. Cook for 5 minutes, then remove from the heat. Set aside.

2. In a saucepan over medium heat, melt the butter. Increase the heat to high, add the tuna, and sear on each side for about 1 minute. Add a pinch of salt. Remove the tuna from the pan but keep the heat on.

3. In the same pan, cook the asparagus on each side for about 1 minute. Add a pinch of salt and remove from the heat.

4. To serve, place the tuna on a plate. Top with the chimichurri and serve with asparagus and bread on the side.

JUVENTUD GUERRERA

FROM **MEXICO CITY, MEXICO** ◆ DEBUT **MARCH 1992**

SON OF LEGENDARY luchador Fuerza Guerrera, Eduardo Aníbal González Hernández, better known by his ring name of Juventud Guerrera, had a similar start to his career in lucha libre as his father. His father was exciting audiences from the moment he entered the ring and within just a few short years was regarded as one of the most talented wrestlers in Mexico. Juventud may have excelled at even a faster rate than his highly respected dad.

Juvy made his debut March 13, 1992, in Hidalgo, Mexico. In less than a year, he debuted with Asistencia Asesoría y Administración (AAA) and began a lengthy and infamous feud with rival Rey Misterio Jr. During the early stages of their feud, we would see Juventud team with his father and wrestle Rey Jr. and his uncle Rey Misterio Sr. There were also tag team matches with father-and-son teams, such as Lizmark and Lizmark Jr. The matches that really put Juventud on the map, though, were his amazing singles matches with Rey Jr.

Just over a year into Juventud's career, he defeated Rey Misterio Jr. for his WWA World Lightweight Championship in Monterrey. They would trade championship wins and losses with each other in matches that would include the WWA Lightweight and Welterweight World Championships.

AAA was doing tremendous business with such talent as Perro Aguayo, Konnan, Los Gringos Locos, and Los Hermanos Dinamita on the top of the cards. One thing that gained AAA a lot of attention internationally was the talent they featured in the middle of the cards. Such young luchadores as Rey Misterio Jr., Psychosis, La Parka, and Juventud Guerrera were introducing fans to a revolutionary, fast-paced style of lucha libre.

In 1996, Juventud's attention in the US would grow as he made his debut for Extreme Championship Wrestling. For many fans in the US, this was their first time watching Guerrera and they were able to witness firsthand his legendary

matches with Rey Jr. The duo had a series of matches in New York and Philadelphia that amazed ECW fans, with tapes of those matches becoming instant favorites of the hard-core fan base and traded worldwide.

Before the end of 1996, Juventud would debut with an even bigger promotion, when he joined Ted Turner's World Championship Wrestling. On August 26, 1996, on an episode of WCW Monday Nitro, Guerrera debuted, defeating Billy Kidman with millions of fans watching at home on television. With Rey Jr. already in WCW, their now-legendary rivalry would continue, and Juventud would often challenge Rey Jr. for his WCW World Cruiserweight Championship. At the time, WCW featured some of the best luchadores and cruiser-weight wrestlers from around the world and their cruiserweight championship was one of the most prestigious titles for lightweight wrestlers in the world.

On January 8, 1998, WCW debuted a new television show called *WCW Thunder*. The first broadcast featured Juventud defeating legendary Japanese wrestler Último Dragón to capture the WCW World Cruiserweight Championship. Although this reign would last only one week, as he would lose it to his archrival Rey Misterio Jr., Juventud would go on to win the championship two more times during his career with WCW.

To a luchador, there is only one thing more valu-able than a championship and that is his mask. And when the stakes need to be raised in a match, the most heated rivalries can lead to apuestas matches where a luchador will "bet" his mask or hair against the mask, hair, or, in this case, championship, of his opponent. At WCW's Super Brawl 8 pay-per-view event in San Francisco, Juventud challenged Cruiserweight champion Chris Jericho to a Mask vs. Title match!

Juventud lost that match and in doing so had to hand his mask to Jericho. He was able to gain some revenge a few months later at another WCW pay-per-view event. This time it took place at WCW's Road Wild event from Sturgis, South Dakota, where he defeated Jericho to capture his second cruiserweight championship.

During his time with WCW, he was given the nickname Juvy and started referring to himself as Juvie-Juice or simply the Juice. It was a nickname that has followed him for the remainder of his career.

After leaving WCW in 2000, he returned to AAA and began making appearances for a variety of promotions around the world, including Japan's Pro Wrestling Noah, the US's Total Nonstop Action, and Mexico's oldest promotion, CMLL.

In 2005, Juventud made his debut with World Wrestling Entertainment. Upon his arrival, he would quickly team with fellow luchadores Psychosis and Super Crazy to form the team known as the Mexicools. The Mexicools quickly became a popular attraction for WWE fans across the globe.

Juvy would soon see gold around his waist again at WWE's No Mercy pay-per-view event on October 9, 2005, where he challenged Nunzio for his WWE Cruiserweight Championship. Juventud was victorious that evening in Houston, Texas, and would hold that title for over a month before losing it to Nunzio in Rome. He would regain it from Nunzio a few weeks later on an episode of *WWE Smackdown* held in Sheffield, England.

After leaving WWE in 2006, Juventud continued to compete internationally and returned to AAA. In May 2012, he competed in a four-way hardcore match at AAA's Noche de Campeones event. That night he defeated Psychosis, Jack Evans, and Teddy Hart to win the AAA Cruiserweight Championship.

Today, Juvy *still* wrestles all across the globe and also runs his own promotion in Mexico called Super X Lucha Libre. And, despite actively competing in the ring for nearly thirty years now, he is *still* a world-class performer and considered one of the best in the game. Fans love watching him wrestle against his most famous rivals as well as taking on today's top up-and-coming stars with whom he can still more than hang.

If you were to make a list of the top twenty-five luchadores who had the greatest impact around the world for the last twenty-five years, Juventud Guerrera would be high on that list. He is also among the group of highly talented luchadores who should be credited with exposing the art of lucha libre to fans all over the world. The success of lucha libre is not where it would be today without the skill shown by Juventud Guerrera and his contemporaries.

COCHINITA PIBIL
(PULLED PORK SHOULDER)

SERVES
2

PORK:

1 pound (455 g) pork shoulder

½ medium-size white onion, sliced

Bay leaves

SAUCE:

½ cup (75 g) guajillo chiles

½ white onion, finely chopped

1.75 ounces (50 g) spiced achiote
   (annatto paste)

2 cups (475 ml) freshly squeezed
   orange juice

½ cup (120 ml) cider vinegar

2 tablespoons (36 g) kosher salt

TO SERVE:

1 medium-size red onion, sliced

4 habanero peppers, seeded,
   deveined, and sliced

1 tablespoon (3 g) oregano

1 tablespoon (15 ml) white vinegar

1 tablespoon (15 ml) freshly
   squeezed lemon juice

Kosher salt

2 small yellow corn tortillas

You've never tasted pulled pork like this. Hailing from the Yucatán, *cochinita pibil* is a unique slow-cooked pork dish with a color as striking as its flavor. While the name of the dish translates as "baby pig," this recipe from Juventud Guerrera is made with easier-to-source and cook pork shoulder.

The pork is tinted a vivid orange due to the addition of annatto seeds; its flavor is equally orangey, thanks to a respectable serving of orange juice in the marinade. It's a surefire favorite among luchadores—and now, in your house too.

1. Make the pork: In a large pot, combine the pork shoulder with the white onion and bay leaves. Fill with enough water to cover the ingredients. Let simmer for 30 minutes, or until cooked through. Remove from the heat, let cool, then shred the meat. Set aside.

2. Make the sauce: In a saucepan, boil the guajillo chiles and onion in 2 cups (475 ml) of water for 20 minutes. Transfer to a blender and add the annatto paste, orange juice, cider vinegar, and salt. Blend until smooth. Pour through a strainer into a large pot.

3. Add the meat and let it sit in the sauce for 1 hour. Then, place the pot over low heat and simmer until ready to serve.

4. In a large bowl, combine the red onion, habanero peppers, oregano, white vinegar, lemon juice, and salt. Set aside, to use as garnish.

5. Cut the tortillas into 2-inch (5 cm) circles; heat briefly on a griddle.
6. To serve, heap the pork shoulder on top of the tortillas and garnish with the onion mixture.

RUGIDO

 MEXICO CITY, MEXICO • **SEPTEMBER 2017**

WITH A MASK that could make him look like a relative of Tiger and Puma King from the Casas dynasty, Rugido (meaning "roar") is a bit of a throwback luchador, having been trained in Olympic and Greco-Roman–style wrestling for over six years before going pro. And while the independent luchador is killer on the ground, Rugido has proven himself to also be a capable high flyer as well. Still in his twenties, as of this writing, the future is bright for this up and comer.

FUN FACTS

* Despite being a masked luchador with an unknown real identity, Rugido has stated that he is the son of Jimmy Jackson, three-time All American Wrestler at Oklahoma State University, former Olympic wrestler, and former pro wrestler in Mid-South Wrestling.

* He was trained in part by the legendary Blue Demon Jr.
* He missed significant time at the start of his career due to a knee injury, but he has not missed a beat since his return.

ENCHILADAS VERDES

MAKES
2

8 tomatillos

¼ medium-size onion

1 to 2 serrano chiles (depending on your desired spice level)

1 garlic clove

1 tablespoon (12 g) chicken bouillon powder

Kosher salt

6 medium-size white corn tortillas

Sour cream

½ chicken breast, cooked and shredded

Grated cheese (queso doble crema, queso Chihuahua, or Mexican Manchego recommended. Monterey Jack can be substituted.)

Rugido's path to lucha libre wrestling may have been round-about and required plenty of discipline, but happily some things in life come easier. For instance . . . these *enchiladas verdes*.

Translated as "green enchiladas," this recipe is extremely easy to make, and the results are incredibly satisfying to the soul. The recipe is a beloved favorite of his, representing one of the family's favorite intimate moments: gathering together on the weekends with a batch of enchiladas and a nice cool glass of soda.

1. In a blender, combine the tomatillos, onion, chiles, garlic, chicken bouillon powder, and salt to taste. Add about 1 cup (240 ml) of water, plus more if necessary, to cover all the ingredients. Blend for 90 seconds, or until the mixture is smooth.

2. Transfer the mixture to a medium-size saucepan over medium-high heat. Add 2 cups (470 ml) of water and bring to a boil. Once boiling, remove the sauce from the heat.

3. To assemble, dip the tortillas in the sauce, then top with shredded chicken and a spoonful of sour cream. Carefully roll. Repeat for the rest of the tortillas, making as many enchiladas as you'd like.

4. Drizzle with any remaining sauce and extra sour cream, and sprinkle with cheese to taste.

LAREDO KID

 NUEVO LAREDO, TAMAULIPAS, MEXICO ◆ **FEBRUARY 2003**

HAILING FROM NUEVO Laredo, Tamaulipas, after competing for a few years in Mexico's independent scene under the name Exterminator, a high-flying luchador signed with Lucha Libre AAA and was given the name Laredo Kid as a way to pay homage to his hometown.

Soon, he would find himself the leader of a group of young técnico luchadores known as Real Fuerza Aérea. The others in the group were Rey Cometa, Super Fly, Nemesis, Aero Star, Pegasso, and El Oriental, many of whom have gone on to become superstars in the industry like Laredo Kid.

In 2011, Laredo Kid left AAA and broke out on his own, not only across Mexico, but across the US as well, wrestling for many top independent companies and earning his reputation as one of the greatest high-flying luchadores of the modern era. The year 2017 would see him join the IMPACT Wrestling roster and be featured on global television for the first time, only further enhancing his reputation—drawing comparisons to a modern day Juventud Guerrera or Psychosis—two legends

who had paved the way for lucha's integration into mainstream pro wrestling in the mid-'90s. Now, Laredo Kid was doing the very same thing some twenty years later at a time when lucha libre was much better understood by the masses.

When he returned to AAA in 2018, he would embark on the greatest run of his career, including winning the AAA Lucha Libre Trios Championships with his Los Jinetes del Aire partners El Hijo del Vikingo and Myzteziz Jr. and winning the Lucha Libre AAA Cruiserweight championship—a title he has held for more than one year as of this writing.

In 2019, Laredo Kid was cast in the reality sports competition series *Exathlon Mexico* and would remain on their island competing week in and week out for many months. Once the luchador was eliminated from the competition, he went right back to the ring as he looked to extend his reign as AAA Cruiserweight Champion and his claim of being one of the most spectacular high flyers and overall best luchadores in the game today.

ENFRIJOLADAS

SERVES
4

½ cup (120 ml) plus 2 tablespoons
    (30 ml) vegetable oil

6 ounces (about 170 g) chorizo

¼ medium-size white onion, finely
    chopped

1 garlic clove, roasted

2 (15.5-ounce [439 g]) cans black
    beans, undrained

1 fresh epazote stalk, with leaves

¾ cup (173 g) sour cream

12 white corn tortillas

1 chicken breast, cooked and
    shredded

8 ounces (225 g) cream cheese

Although he originally hails from Nuevo Laredo, Laredo Kid's luchador career has taken him all across Mexico and the US. Along the way, he picked up this traditional central Mexican recipe for enfrijoladas, a popular platter featuring meat-filled rolled tortillas with a mélange of tasty toppings.

You don't have double vision: There are, in fact, two enfrijoladas recipes in this book. However, there are some distinct differences between this recipe and Estrellita's enfrijoladas (page 124).

Whereas the other recipe features chicken and pinto beans, this version features black beans scented with epazote and a fried chorizo garnish, giving it a distinctly different finished flavor. It just goes to show how truly adaptable and customizable this dish can be.

1. In a medium-size saucepan, combine 1 tablespoon (15 ml) of the oil and the chorizo. Cook for 3 to 5 minutes over medium-high heat until the chorizo reaches an internal temperature of 160°F (71°C). Remove from the heat and set aside.

2. In a large saucepan over medium heat, combine 1 tablespoon (15 ml) of oil with the onion and garlic and cook until browned. Add the beans (with liquid) and epazote stalk. Cook for 10 minutes. Remove from the heat and transfer to a blender. Add the sour cream. Blend until smooth.

3. Transfer the mixture back to its saucepan and place over low heat to keep it warm.

4. In a separate medium-size or large saucepan, heat the remaining ½ cup (120 ml) of oil over medium heat. Once hot, add the tortillas, one at a time, and fry quickly, about 30 seconds per side.

5. One at a time, dip the tortillas in the bean sauce to lightly coat them. Once coated, spoon a line of shredded chicken down the center of each tortilla, then roll each into a cylinder.

6. Serve three enfrijoladas per plate. Top with additional bean sauce, cream cheese, and fried chorizo. Serve hot.

What is epazote?

This is a Mexican aromatic herb/tea plant that can be used in cooking. In this recipe, you'll use the entire stalk, including the leaves. You can find it online or in the spice section of many grocery stores. Others may carry it in their Hispanic foods section.

ESTRELLITA

 ZAMORA, MICHOCÁN, MEXICO • **FEBRUARY 1993**

BORN BIBIANA OCHOA Barradas, Estrellita followed in the footsteps of her grandfather, Rafael Barradas, and became a luchadora at the age of fifteen in 1993. Only a few years later, she would join Lucha Libre AAA, but despite her skill, she spent most of her twelve-year stint with the promotion as an undercard *técnica*. Fortunes changed when she joined CMLL in 2010. Since then, Estrellita has been one of the top stars of the promotion's luchadoras division, holding the Mexican National Women's Championship for over two years and defeating Amapola in a Hair vs. Hair match at Homenaje a Dos Leyendas 2013. Even with decades of experience under her belt, having started so young, Estrellita looks to have many more years in front of her entertaining the fans of Arena México.

FUN FACTS

* Before becoming a luchadora, Estrellita played keyboard in a band called Los Rudos del Ritmo, made up of famous luchadores, including Ari Romero, Gran Apache, and Kung Fu.

* She was heavily featured in the 2018 docu-reality series *Nuestra Lucha Libre*, which focused on many luchadores who worked for CMLL.
* Back in the '90s, she was nicknamed "The Britney Spears of Lucha Libre."

ENFRIJOLADAS "GÜERAS"

MAKES
2
enchiladas

4¼ cups (about 1 L) frijoles de la
olla (prepared bean stew)

3 chiles de arbol

2 avocado leaves (MexGrocer and
Walmart both sell online)

Vegetable oil, for pan

Medium-size white corn tortillas

½ chicken breast, cooked and
shredded

¼ cup (60 g) sour cream

½ cup (60 g) grated cheese
(Chihuahua cheese or Mexican
Manchego recommended.
Monterey Jack can be
substituted.)

My mother, Estrellita, has enjoyed a storied career as a luchadora and she's enjoyed plenty of achievements and accolades. But on a personal level, what brings her the greatest joy is spending time with her family.

Being a successful luchadora and a single mother of two children isn't easy. Plus, she's currently studying medicine with the hope of becoming a neurosurgeon! But she still makes time for family. She chose to share this dish because it's easy to make and it's one of her favorite meals to enjoy with me and my brother.

1. In a blender, combine the frijoles, chiles de arbol, and avocado leaves. Blend until smooth. The mixture will be thick.
2. In a large saucepan with a light coating of oil, fry the tortillas for about 30 seconds on each side to attain a golden color, but don't let them get crispy.
3. Fill the fried tortillas with the shredded chicken breast, roll them into cylinders, and spoon the sauce on top; drizzle with sour cream and sprinkle with cheese to taste.

Frijoles de la Olla

Translated, frijoles de la olla simply means "beans in a pot." This humble dish, made with beans and aromatics, is considered a foundational dish in Mexican cooking. It acts as the basis for many dishes including refried beans and enfrijoladas. While an "olla" or clay pot is traditional, they can be made in any type of pot or even a slow cooker!

PREP: SHRED CHICKEN.

AL LOWDON

FROM **LONDON, ENGLAND**

THE GROWTH OF lucha libre across the world is evidenced by the popularity of luchadores in Europe. As a longtime fan of professional wrestling, Al Lowdon began writing articles for the lucha libre zine *Rudo Can't Fail*. With the increase of luchadores being booked by promotions in the UK, Al reached out to Masked Republic owners about the potential of opening an office to serve customers in Europe.

The desire for merchandise and lucha-based brands have increased dramatically over the years. With the increase in demand for merchandise, Al saw a great opportunity to present world-class officially licensed products that are produced by Masked Republic to the fans in European countries.

This inquiry led to Al being named the general manager of Masked Republic Europe. As general manager, Al helps push awareness of events and merchandise from the company as well as publish news, including news from its partner promotions. He also develops relationships with luchadores who are based in Europe.

Over the last decade, entire wrestling promotions based around lucha libre have been formed throughout the European continent. Many of them will bring in top stars from Mexico to headline their events.

Al's goal as general manager is to bring lucha libre to an even larger platform. He can see the presence of Masked Republic growing in Europe by introducing the company's brands to the fan base, including Legends of Lucha Libre officially licensed products, clothing brand RUDA Lifestyle, comic book world The Luchaverse, and fan convention Expo Lucha.

FISH PIE

SERVES
4 to 6

1 pound (455 g) cod and/or smoked
   haddock

Kosher salt and freshly ground
   black pepper

4 tablespoons (½ stick, 55 g)
   unsalted butter

¼ cup (30 g) all-purpose flour

½ medium-size white onion,
   chopped into ¼-inch (6 mm)
   pieces

1 bay leaf

14 ounces (414 ml) whole milk

6 ounces (170 g) prawns, head,
   legs, shells, and veins removed

4 hard-boiled eggs, cut lengthwise
   into quarters

4 ounces (110 g) frozen peas,
   defrosted

1 tablespoon (4 g) chopped fresh
   parsley

1 pound (455 g) prepared mashed
   potatoes

When Masked Republic general manager Al Lowdon left home, his grandmother was apparently fearful that he might starve once left to his own devices. To prevent this worrisome fate, she gifted him with a fat stack of recipes.

This fish pie was among them, and it remains a fond memory of his grandmother—and what Al calls, "in my opinion, one of the ultimate comfort foods."

NOTE: Although cod and smoked haddock are called for in this recipe, any other firm fish, such as halibut, smoked salmon, or pollack can be substituted.

1. Position a rack in the middle of the oven. Preheat the oven to 400°F (200°C).

2. In a large, deep baking dish (about 7 x 11 inches [18 x 28 cm], 2½ inches [6.5 cm] deep), sprinkle salt and pepper on the fish. Bake for 10 to 12 minutes, until flaky, or until an internal thermometer reaches 145°F (63°C). Remove from the oven and set aside to cool. Once cool enough to touch, discard any skin and bones and break the fish into large chunks, keeping them in the same pan.

3. While the fish is cooking, make the white sauce for the pie: Place 2 tablespoons (28 g) of the butter and all the flour in a large, deep skillet or saucepan. Add the onion and bay leaf.

4. Gradually whisk in the milk and bring the mixture to a boil, stirring constantly to keep the mixture from clumping or sticking to the bottom of the pan. Once boiling, cook for 3 to 4 minutes, or until thickened. Discard the bay leaf and onion.

5. Add the prawns, quartered eggs, peas, parsley, and white sauce mixture to the fish in the baking dish.

6. Cover the mixture with the mashed potatoes and dot the remaining 2 tablespoons (57 g) of butter on top.

7. Bake until the top of the pie has browned and the juices are bubbling at the sides, about 25 minutes. Serve immediately!

LÁTIGO

 MEXICO CITY, MEXICO ✦ **FEBRUARY 2012**

ONCE UPON A time, Látigo was a Ninja Turtle. I'm not joking! Trained by the likes of Black Terry, Negro Navarro, and Los Traumas, Látigo initially burst onto the scene as a member of Los Tortugas Ninjas, a stable of luchadores loosely portraying members of the *Teenage Mutant Ninja Turtles*. As Leo, Látigo was the leader of the group, until he shed the half shell in 2015 for the name he began his career with. Now splitting his time between Lucha Libre AAA and the indies, Látigo has arguably developed into one of the best rudos in lucha libre, known for his creativity and impeccable basing (on the receiving end of high-flying moves).

FUN FACTS

* Stunningly, Látigo has never held a championship in his career, even as a Ninja Turtle!
* He's worked for North American promotion IMPACT Wrestling while it did shows in Mexico, and also briefly worked for Oriental Wrestling Entertainment (OWE) in China, where he received additional training from the legendary CIMA.
* He always carries an Indiana Jones–style bullwhip with him to the ring because "Látigo" translates to "whip."

FRIED FISH

SERVES
4

6 ounces (175 ml) Corona beer

2 cups (250 g) all-purpose flour

1 tablespoon (9 g) garlic powder

4 teaspoons (8 g) freshly ground
   black pepper

2 teaspoons (9 g) kosher salt

1 tablespoon (12 g) chicken
   bouillon powder

Small pinch of baking soda

Small pinch of baking powder

About 2 cups (475 ml) vegetable
   oil, or enough to fully submerge
   the fish

2¼ pounds (1 kg) tilapia fillets, cut
   into strips

Serving Suggestion

Serve with lettuce, lemon, and
Valentina sauce (or other hot sauce
of your choosing).

Sometimes, the simplest foods provide the purest pleasure.
This recipe is nostalgic for independent luchador Látigo: as
a child, he would spend time with his grandmother by the
seaside—that's where he learned how to prepare this fried
fish dish.

Mild-flavored tilapia is the perfect base for a richly flavored
beer batter, which yields a pleasingly crispy fried exterior. A
simple side salad and hot sauce round out the meal, making
for a wonderful but simple and unfussy dish to prepare.

1. In a blender, combine 1 cup (240 ml) of water with the beer,
   flour, garlic powder, pepper, salt, chicken bouillon powder,
   baking soda, and baking powder. Blend until the ingredients are
   well mixed; the mixture will be thick. Transfer to a shallow bowl
   and set aside.

2. In a medium-size or large pot, heat the oil for about 10 minutes
   over high heat, or until it reaches a frying temperature between
   350° and 375°F (177° and 191°C).

3. Dip the fish strips into the flour mixture one by one, making
   sure to coat them evenly and on all sides. Immediately after
   coating, drop into the hot oil and fry for 3 to 5 minutes. The
   oil should be able to submerge the fish completely; if not, add
   more and let it heat up before proceeding.

4. After 3 to 5 minutes, or once browned and crispy on both sides, remove the fish from the oil. Blot any excess oil with paper towels. Repeat with the remaining portions of tilapia until all the fish is cooked.
5. Serve with chopped lettuce, lemon wedges, and Valentina sauce.

What is Valentina sauce?

It's a popular hot sauce in Mexico, made by the Guadalajara-based company Salsa Tamazula. No self-respecting luchador is without a bottle of this hot stuff, which is pourable in texture and adds some pleasing heat to just about any dish. It's readily found in the Hispanic aisle of most grocery stores, but should you have trouble locating it, your favorite hot sauce will do just fine.

ADRIAN SALAS

 **SAN DIEGO, CA**

LIKE SO MANY involved with the world of lucha libre, Adrian Salas was born into it. His grandmother is Guadalupe Ramirez (see page 40) and his grandfather is legendary luchador Super Astro (see page 138). Some of his earliest memories are of being in the Auditorio de Tijuana. His grandma and aunt would go to the rear locker room and Adrian would get to sit and watch the matches with his great-grandmother sitting in the second level of the arena. Well, technically, he was "banned" to the second level of the arena ever since he jumped into the ring in the middle of a match.

It was not something that he intended to do—interrupt an actual lucha match in progress. It's actually very common for lucha libre shows to allow kids to get into the ring and play around *after* the matches. Young Adrian thought the matches were over and he hit the ring. It turns out, he was wrong. The luchadores and ref had left the ring as they battled on the outside, and he slipped in. All

of a sudden, people were screaming at him, and the next thing he knew, he was surrounded by six rather large men. One of the masked luchadores said to him in Spanish, "Adriáncito, get out!" He was shocked that this superstar knew his name, but he didn't have too much time to stare in awe as his dad pulled him out of the ring. And that was the last time, as a child, he was allowed in the lower level of the arena.

Adrian's dad and cousins would walk around the ring in matching T-shirts to act as ringside security of sorts, making sure nobody could jump in. And after the shows, they were always the last people out of the arena, which Adrian found annoying since all the vendors outside were gone and they would end up going to eat Chinese food at their house with twenty-plus people. They always had people over with weird names—people named El Patas, El Mongol, and El Pocho, to name a few. It was only later that Adrian would find out that they were luchadores. On the days that luchadores didn't come to his house, he was usually heading to one of their houses with his aunt or grandmother. And then the weekend would come and it was luchas, luchas, luchas.

One of Adrian's most vivid memories of a match was a very intense battle his grandpa and uncle were in. His grandpa's mask was torn to shreds and he could tell that his head was all bloody. But in the calm, after the fans had gone, they walked out as if nothing had happened. Not that they weren't injured, but they were tough! Adrian was always scared of his uncle because he was a *rudo*—like a textbook *rudo*. He would fight dirty and yell at the crowd.

Adrian was born too late to really be part of the golden era of his grandmother's promotion, Promociones Internacionales. His lucha education came from stories his aunt Lourdes would tell him or from his dad, such as about how he would train in Jesse Garcia's backyard and the now historic Gil's Gym in Los Angeles. When his aunt Leti and uncle Martin (known in lucha libre as El Zorro de Oro, the Golden Fox, and Antichristo) moved back to San Diego from Mexico, Adrian was so excited. Finally, an active luchador member of his family would be local. But when he spoke with his uncle, he told him that there was no more money in lucha libre and that he had stopped four years earlier.

Through the years as Adrian got older, his grandma got more and more sick. He would spend the summers in LA with family, including his uncle Martin who would take him to lucha events. In his early twenties, several years after his grandmother had passed away, his grandfather, Super Astro, came back into his life. One of the most revolutionary luchadores of the 1980s, Astro was back from Mexico City, working between Tijuana and LA. It was through conversations with luchadores at these events that Adrian learned much more about his legendary grandma.

After his uncle Martin passed away, Adrian went to Los Angeles for his burial. It was only then that he was able to really see photos and hear detailed stories that illustrated for him just how big a star the Golden Fox was in Tijuana. He heard all about his uncle Martin's matches in Mexico, including his main event feud with Rey Misterio Sr. and their Mask vs. Mask match.

A few months later, Adrian learned that another influential luchador in his family's history, Tury González, had passed away. Adrian found himself very saddened beyond the loss of a friend. He was realizing that the legends of Tijuana, and their amazing stories, were starting to fade. This was followed closely by the news that his grandfather was in the hospital in Mexico City but was having financial difficulties to pay for his needed surgery. Adrian could not believe that someone who had been such a star would still have trouble paying for a life-saving procedure. Still wracked with guilt over not making it to LA to visit his uncle before he passed, Adrian quit his job of fifteen years and dedicated himself to figuring out how to raise money for his grandfather's surgery.

The "print on demand" boom was just starting to take off and launching a store with Amazon would allow Adrian to offer T-shirts without having to pay for and stock inventory. A quick pitch to his grandfather and Golden Era Lucha Tees was born.

The two started collaborating on ideas and before long Super Astro's hospital bills were covered. Shortly after, Adrian saw a Facebook post about a benefit show in LA for luchador turned promoter Falcon de Oro. He attended the event and reconnected with a number of LA lucha legends. Tragically, in the middle of the main event match, news came in that Falcon de Oro had just passed away in the hospital. Super Boy (see page 152) got in the ring and told of the hardship that Falcon de Oro had gone through and the determination he'd had to get lucha libre into the US.

That night, Adrian was completely inspired and wanted to do more, partly because helping luchadores is what his grandmother did and partly because he wanted to preserve history and tell stories. Luchadores Terremoto Quintero and El Pocho helped line up legends for Adrian. Soon, members of the lucha media and more stars were on board too.

These days, Adrian continues to help the stars create T-shirts, and whatever else he can do to lend a hand, be it simply helping them network or trying to get their incredible stories told.

GARLIC SHRIMP

SERVES

4

¼ cup (60 ml) extra-virgin olive oil

1 medium-size white onion, julienned

2 medium-size tomatoes, sliced ½ inch (1.3 cm) thick

1 green bell pepper, seeded and julienned

4 cups (80 g) fresh cilantro, chopped

1 teaspoon (5 ml) chicken bouillion powder

Kosher salt

6 to 12 garlic cloves, minced

1 pound shrimp (455 g), deveined and peeled, tails removed

Freshly ground black pepper

Serving Suggestion

This recipe pairs nicely with white rice and salad.

Adrian Salas comes from a lucha family—his grandmother is promoter Guadalupe Ramirez (see page 40) and his grandfather is legendary luchador Super Astro (see page 138). While he's still in the family biz, Adrian stays on the artistic side, as the proprietor of Golden Era Lucha Tees. He's also an accomplished graphic designer who has created works of art for his grandfather's restaurants.

This recipe is from his grandmother, who passed away when he was eighteen years old. For him, it evokes the energy and memory of a different time, when his dad and cousins would walk around the lucha ring in matching T-shirts as a kind of makeshift security unit.

This aromatic dish, featuring garlicky shrimp and richly seasoned bell peppers, is the perfect way to refuel after a match—or, you know, any time.

1. In a saucepan, heat 3 tablespoons (45 ml) of the oil over medium heat. Add the onion, tomatoes, and bell pepper and cook for 5 minutes. Add the chopped cilantro, chicken bouillon powder, and salt to taste.

2. In a separate saucepan over medium heat in the remaining tablespoon (15 ml) of oil, sauté the garlic and shrimp until fully cooked, about 5 minutes. Add salt and black pepper to taste.

3. Transfer the shrimp and garlic to the pan that contains the onion mixture. Cook over medium heat for about 2 minutes. Serve warm.

SUPER ASTRO

 TIJUANA, BAJA CALIFORNIA, MEXICO ♦ **MAY 1974**

NOW KNOWN FOR his incredible *tortas* (sandwiches on rolls or buns) today as he was well known as a luchador, Super Astro has entertained fans of lucha libre for many decades. Born Juan Zezatti Ramirez in Tijuana, Baja California, on October 1, 1961, Astro began his career in lucha libre at only thirteen years old and was considered something of a wrestling savant from an early age. When he broke in, he wrestled under a variety of names, including Rey Bucanero and Pequeño Apolo. At the age of eighteen, he took the name Super Astro and started wearing a mask covered in stars that has become his calling card for decades.

After gaining experience around the Baja California territory, he was brought into the Mexico City–based UWA promotion, one of the largest companies in the world. In November 1983, Francisco Flores brought him into El Toreo de Cuatro Caminos, which was one of lucha libre's biggest hotbeds for wrestling anywhere in the world. Shortly after arriving he was teamed with Solar and Ultraman as a trio that would go on to be known as Los Cadetes del Espacio, or simply the Space Cadets.

The Space Cadets were instant favorites among fans of lucha libre. Trios matches of teams with similar identities were becoming all the rage in lucha libre and Los Cadetes del Espacio were among the favorites, with their unique high-flying manuevers and space age–looking masks. Nearly every week, they would be placed into matches with other trios units, such as Hall of Fame team Los Misioneros de la Muerte: El Signo, El Texano, and Negro Navarro. Or Los Temararios, Los Brazos, or the exótico team of La Ola Lila (the Lilac Wave). Or the team that was possibly their biggest rivals of the era, the trio of Kato Kung Lee, Black Man, and Kung Fu: Los Fantasticos.

It was Los Fantasticos that defeated Los Cadetes del Espacio on March 18, 1984, at El Toreo de Cautro Caminos in Naucalpan to capture the first-ever UWA World Trios Championship. After numerous opportunities, it was a championship

the Cadets were never able to capture, but they were part of a legacy that would last longer than the UWA, as trios matches became the standard at lucha libre events throughout Mexico and still are for CMLL and AAA today.

Despite not capturing the trios championship, 1984 was a great year in the career of Super Astro. On July 6, 1984, in Guadalajara, he faced Gran Hamada for his UWA World Middleweight Championship. In the third fall of a spectacular match, Super Astro was able to defeat Gran Hamada for his title and capture the most prestigious championship of his career.

He followed that up two days later at El Toreo in Naucalpan, when he and his partners Solar and Ultraman placed their masks on the line against the hair of Black Terry, Jose Luis Feliciano, and El Lobo Rubio in a trios apuestas match. They defeated their opponents and took the hair of Los Temerarios at the nearly full bullring.

One of Super Astro's more renowned matches of his career was one that he did not win. It took place Christmas night of 1999 in his hometown, at the famous Auditorio de Tijuana. The match was advertised as a "relevos suicidas" match. Stipulations of this match called for the losing team to face each other in an apuestas match, putting up their masks or hair. The teams were Fishman and Lizmark to face Villano III and Super Astro. Super Astro's team lost the match, forcing the team members to put their mask up against each other. And unfortunately, Super Astro was not successful in his match with Villano III and thus had to remove his mask and reveal his identity.

Despite losing the match, Super Astro would later state that the promoter never paid him for losing his mask, and so he would return to wearing it in matches and at his world-famous torta restaurant.

The unique style of lucha libre Super Astro brought to rings in Mexico has inspired a generation of luchadores who have come after him. As the brother-in-law of luchador Rey Misterio, and because he often competed in Tijuana, he became a favorite of Rey Misterio Jr., better known these days as the WWE's Rey Mysterio. The famous 6-1-9 move that the former WWE World Champion made famous was inspired by watching Super Astro. Rey Mysterio has publicly stated that he was inspired by the legend and borrowed some of his ring mannerisms and moves from him.

Outside the ring, Super Astro has been part of six different lucha-themed restaurants over the last four decades (the first four were founded with Guadalupe, his wife at the time):

Puerto Vallarta, San Ysidro, CA, 1984

Puerto Vallarta, Tijuana, Baja, CA, 1989

El Cuadrilátero, Mexico City, 1992 (now run by his ex-wife and his son Super Astro Jr.)

El Cuadrilátero de la Tortas, Tijuana, 2006

Tortas Super Astro, Mexico City, 2012 (relocated to a larger location in 2016)

El Cuadrilátero de Súper Astro, Ixtapaluca, 2019

GLADIATOR TORTA

MAKES
6-pound
sandwich

1 (15-inch) baguette, sliced in half
   lengthwise

Mayonnaise

1 large tomato, sliced

1 large avocado, peeled, pitted,
   and sliced

1 medium-size onion, sliced

½ cup (72 g) sliced jalapeño
   peppers

5 slices (about 1¾ pounds [800 g])
   ham

7 ounces (200 g) queso Oaxaca or
   buffalo mozzarella

1¾ pounds (800 g) longaniza or
   chorizo

8 large eggs

1¾ pounds (800 g) chicken breast

1¾ pounds (800 g) flank steak

1¾ pounds (800 g) bacon

1¾ pounds (800 g) bratwurst or hot
   dogs

Super Astro eats like he fights—gladiator-style! He gained a reputation for his appetite while working with Ari Romero—their epic buffet binges became the stuff of legends in the luchador world.

Years later, when Super Astro and Baby Face opened up a restaurant and Romero came in as a customer, they knew that only a truly epic sandwich would satisfy Romero's appetite. The local *panaderia* was out of traditional bolillo rolls, so they used an entire baguette instead. Piled high with toppings, the finished product weighed as much as a newborn baby and was dubbed El Gladiador.

The sandwich was a fast success and was added to the menu; for a mere US equivalent of $15, you can enjoy all 6 pounds (2.6 kg) of it for yourself at any of Super Astro's Mexico City restaurants. Or, on certain days and times, you can try the Gladiator Challenge—eat the whole thing in fifteen minutes or less and it's free!

Of course, if you're not a sucker for gluttony, you may prefer the more petite Gladiator Jr. recipe, which uses about a third of the resources required for the full-size version (page 145).

1. Prepare the baguette: Spread mayo generously on both halves and top with tomato, avocado, onion, and sliced jalapeño to your liking. Layer slices of ham and Oaxaca cheese on top. Set the sandwich aside for the moment.

RECIPE CONTINUED >

2. In a large saucepan (no oil), fry the chorizo for 3 to 5 minutes over medium heat until browned and cooked through. Once cooked, add the eggs. Cook omelet style, browning one side and then flipping to brown the second side to match.

3. In separate saucepans, fry the chicken breast, steak, bacon, and bratwurst.

4. Pile the cooked meats on top of the prepared sandwich halves, stack it all together, and enjoy.

WEIGHS AS MUCH as a newborn baby!

STEP FOUR: STACK IT ALL TOGETHER.

SUPER ASTRO JR.

 MEXICO CITY, MEXICO ◆ **AUGUST 2014**

IN SOME WAYS Super Astro Jr. has it made. His theme music is the *Star Wars* theme; he was brought aboard CMLL after only four years as a professional luchador; and his father, Super Astro, is both a legendary luchador and a guy who knows where to get you some darn good tortas at a moment's notice. Oh, and Super Astro Jr. was also trained by his father and other legendary luchadores, such as Solar, Virus, and Lizmark. It shows; the luchador in his early twenties may still be on the lower end of CMLL cards, but already he displays the technical skill of Solar and Virus and the exciting high flying ability of Lizmark and his father. It's those skills that helped make the young Astro Lucha Central's 2018 Rookie of the Year, an award that will probably not be the last one he wins before his career winds down.

FUN FACTS

★ Super Astro Jr. debuted for CMLL as part of the Copa Nuevo Valores tournament.

★ Originally wrestled under the name King Star before joining CMLL.

★ Teamed with his father for the first time in trios action at a show for The Crash in 2019, where the father/son duo teamed with Mr. Iguana to defeat Arandú, Star Boy, and Zarco.

GLADIATOR JR.

MAKES
3-pound
sandwich

1 (7½-inch [19 cm]) length of baguette, sliced in half lengthwise

Mayonnaise

½ large tomato, sliced

½ large avocado, peeled, pitted, and sliced

½ medium-size onion, sliced

¼ cup (36 g) sliced jalapeño peppers

2 ounces (55 g) ham, sliced

4 ounces (115 g) queso Oaxaca

5.5 ounces (150 g) chorizo

4 large eggs

5.5 ounces (150 g) chicken breast

5.5 ounces (150 g) flank steak

4 slices bacon

5.5 ounces (150 g) bratwurst or hot dogs

Super Astro Jr., winner of the Lucha Central Rookie of the Year award for 2018, has not only come into his own as an accomplished luchador in CMLL but has taken up the family business of creating generously sized sandwiches too.

He and his mother now run El Cuadrilátero, the original family restaurant in Mexico City. There, in addition to the original Gladiator Torta (see page 141), eaters with lighter appetites can opt for the smaller (yet still pretty darn big) Gladiator Jr., which is about half the size of the original. The instructions are the same, but the recipe uses half the bread and adjusts the various proteins to smaller quantities.

1. Prepare the baguette. Spread mayo generously on both halves and top with tomato, avocado, onion, and sliced jalapeño to your liking. Layer slices of ham and Oaxaca cheese on top. Set the sandwich aside for the moment.

2. In a large saucepan (no oil), fry the chorizo for 3 to 5 minutes over medium heat until browned and cooked through. Once cooked, add the eggs. Cook omelet style, browning one side and then flipping to brown the second side to match.

3. In separate saucepans, fry the chicken breast, steak, bacon, and bratwurst.

4. Pile the cooked meats on top of the prepared sandwich halves, stack it all together, and enjoy.

IMPULSO

 MEXICO CITY, MEXICO ◆ **OCTOBER 2003**

TRAINED BY LEGENDARY "maestro de maestros" (teacher of teachers) Black Terry, Impulso initially began his career as the masked luchador Yagan. He quickly traded the mask for his now more famous name and eventually broke out on the independents as a member of Los Indystrongtibles, a popular trio also consisting of Belial and current Lucha Libre AAA star Arez. Known for their high flying and creativity while also maintaining an edge as dastardly rudos, Los Indystrongtibles is widely considered one of the most exciting trios teams to come out of the independent scene in the 2010s. While still teaming occasionally these days, Impulso has largely become a star on his own, and he remains a luchador that will come at you from everywhere with his devastating splash to the floor.

FUN FACTS

* Impulso is a former XWM Junior Heavyweight Champion and AKE Cruiserweight Champion.

* Biggest match to date was a Hair vs. Hair match against Freelance (Lucha Libre AAA's Laredo Boy) in June 2016, which Impulso won.
* His name translates as "impulse."

HíGADO A LA CERVEZA (BEER LIVER TACOS)

SERVES
4

2 tablespoons (30 ml) vegetable oil, plus more to cover the liver

1 medium-size white onion, chopped (about 1 cup [160 g])

2 serrano peppers, seeds removed

2 medium-size tomatoes, sliced

2¼ pounds (1 kg) beef liver, cut into strips

2 teaspoons (12 g) kosher salt

2 teaspoons (6 g) garlic powder

1 (12-ounce [355 ml]) bottle of beer

8 to 10 medium-size tortillas

SAUCE:

1 serrano pepper, seeds removed

2 teaspoons (about 10 g) kosher salt

¼ white onion, sliced

4 medium-size tomatoes

1 garlic clove

Food is about memories. Mexico City–born luchador Impulso comes from a family of professional wrestlers and recalls that on occasions when friends gathered at his house, his father would prepare this dish for the crowd. For him, this recipe is forever linked with good times and great company.

These days, Impulso creates this fragrant and richly flavored dish with his brothers while they reminisce about the good times shared with their father. What memories will you create when you make this dish?

1. In a deep saucepan, heat 2 tablespoons (30 ml) of vegetable oil and fry the onion and peppers for about 7 minutes, or until the onion has become translucent and golden.

2. Add the tomato slices to the pan and mix in with the onion and peppers.

3. Add the liver and enough oil to make sure that the liver is fully covered, cover the pan, and cook for 5 minutes. Add the salt and garlic powder. Cover again and cook for 6 more minutes.

4. Give it a taste; add more salt, if desired. Add the beer and mix all the ingredients with a spatula. Cover and cook for 10 minutes, or until thickened.

5. Make the sauce: In a blender, combine all the sauce ingredients. Pulse until the mixture is blended but remains chunky.

6. Transfer to a small pot and bring to a boil. Let cool slightly.

7. To serve, pile the liver mixture on tortillas and serve with sauce.

LIL' CHOLO

 ORANGE COUNTY, CA ◆ **OCTOBER 1998**

A VETERAN OF THE Southern California independent scene and a member of the short-lived Wrestling Society X series on MTV globally, Lil' Cholo's breakthrough came a good fifteen years into his career and under a different name. Signed by *Lucha Underground* in 2014, he soon became known as Mr. Cisco, a street fighter as part of the villainous stable The Crew. Lil' Cholo would go on to play several roles in LU before the end of the show (including a stint as Rabbit Tribe member Mala Suerte), but no matter what, he always impressed with some great brawling and surprising athleticism. Still killing it in California, Lil' Cholo has reverted back to his own persona but has kept hanging out with fellow LU alumnus and former Rabbit Tribe member Mariachi Loco, forming the entertaining tag team known as The Lucha Homies (see Mariachi Loco's story and recipe on pages 250–252).

FUN FACTS

* Along with his Lucha Homie Mariachi Loco, Lil' Cholo is the only Lucha Underground performer to have been "killed off" twice during the show's run. Maybe that's what bonded them into becoming such homies.

* Lil' Cholo has held six championships, including the Lucha VaVOOM Championship.
* He was an early member of the Pro Wrestling Guerrilla roster, wrestling the likes of Frankie Kazarian (IMPACT, AEW), Rocky Romero (NJPW), and TJ Perkins (WWE, IMPACT).

HUEVOS DIVORCIADOS

SERVES
2

HUEVOS DIVORCIADOS:

2 tablespoons (30 ml) vegetable oil, plus more if needed

4 medium-size white corn tortillas

4 large eggs

1 cup (260 g) green salsa (recipe follows)

1 cup (260 g) red salsa (recipe follows)

TO SERVE:

1 cup (238 g) refried beans

¼ cup (60 g) queso doble crema or cream cheese

About 8 tortilla chips, for garnish

Salt and freshly ground black pepper

Huevos divorciados may translate to "divorced eggs," but truthfully, this recipe is all about the marriage of red and green salsa. A delicious mess of ingredients, including eggs, beans, and cheese, is generously topped with a little bit of two types of salsa, making for an incredible meal. No need for a custody battle here: it all tastes good!

This recipe is the perfect reflection of luchador Lil' Cholo, who is a study in contrasts. In his career, he's been both the *rudo* (bad guy) and *técnico* (good guy). He's wrestled on TV in front of millions, but he still makes time to go back to small venues to pay homage to where he came from. Is it any surprise that his favorite dish has two distinct sides too?

1. In a saucepan, heat 2 tablespoons (30 ml) of vegetable oil. Working one at a time, fry the tortillas for about 15 seconds on each side, long enough so that they are golden but not totally browned. Replenish the oil as needed. Remove the tortillas from the pan and set aside.

2. Using the same pan, cook the eggs sunny-side up, cooking over medium-low heat for 3 to 5 minutes, or until the egg white is cooked through.

3. To serve, place two tortillas on each plate. Top each tortilla evenly with an egg. Add ½ cup (130 g) each of green salsa and red salsa on top of the egg on each plate so each plate has one green and one red portion. Serve the beans and cream cheese on the side. Garnish with tortilla chips; add salt and pepper to taste.

What is queso doble crema?

Translated as "double cream cheese," this is a rich, buttery, and creamy-textured cheese. If you're unable to find it in your grocery store, you can substitute American cream cheese.

GREEN SALSA

4 to 6 tomatillos, cut into quarters

3 serrano peppers, stems removed

1/8 medium-size white onion, finely chopped

1 bunch cilantro

Salt and freshly ground black pepper

1. In a saucepan, combine the tomatillos, serrano peppers, and onion over medium heat. Cover with enough water to submerge the ingredients. Bring the mixture to a boil for 15 minutes. Transfer the mixture to a blender, adding the cilantro. Blend until smooth; season to taste with salt and black pepper. If the mixture is too thick for your liking, add a little water.

RED SALSA

3 serrano peppers, stems removed

1 garlic clove, minced

2 Roma tomatoes

Salt and freshly ground black pepper

1. In a saucepan, grill the serrano peppers and garlic over medium-high heat for 10 to 15 minutes. Turn the peppers frequently so that they get grilled on all sides. If you prefer your salsa less spicy, remove the seeds from the peppers before proceeding.

2. Transfer the peppers and garlic to a blender; add the tomatoes. Blend until the mixture has reached your desired consistency. Season with salt and black pepper to taste.

SUPER BOY

 GUADALAJARA, JALISCO, MEXICO ♦ **DECEMBER 1987**

FEW LUCHADORES HAVE the back story of Sergio Torres, aka Super Boy. Born in Mexico, Super Boy was raised in California after his family moved when he was only two years old. At three, he was rolling around in the ring, already inspired to follow his father, El Moro, and brothers Capitán Oro and Príncipe Hindú in becoming a luchador. He would go on to debut at nineteen years old in 1987, and instead of going to Mexico he stayed in California to become a local star. All this led to Super Boy getting booked in Japan with the newly formed Michinoku Pro Wrestling in 1993; he would wrestle there for ten years and would even go on to win the WWA World Middleweight Championship during his run. Returning to the US for good in 2003, Super Boy would work between California and Mexico before settling into a part-time role, wrestling his last match in July 2015.

FUN FACTS

* Super Boy was a member of the Kaientai DX with Dick Togo, Gran Hamada, Shoichi Funaki, and TAKA Michinoku. Togo, Funaki, and TAKA would all go on to wrestle as Kaientai for WWF during the late '90s.
* Although mostly based in the US and Japan, Super Boy did work sparingly for major lucha promotions, wrestling once for AAA in the '90s and a few times for the International Wrestling Revolution Group (IWRG) between 1997 and 1998.
* He took part in the recently uncovered WCW Festival de Lucha tapings in 1999; he teamed with El Felino and Villano V to take on Kendo, Silver King, and Venum in a losing effort.

SUPER BOY JR.

HUEVOS RANCHEROS

SERVES
2

SALSA:

3 medium-size tomatoes

2 serrano chiles

¼ medium-size white onion, finely chopped

½ garlic clove, finely chopped

1 tablespoon (15 ml) vegetable oil

Kosher salt

EGGS AND GARNISH:

¼ cup (605 ml) vegetable oil

4 medium-size corn tortillas

4 large eggs

9 ounces (255 g) refried beans

Tortilla chips

Who made it best? According to luchador Super Boy, huevos rancheros was the source of some friction in his household while he was growing up.

His father loved this dish when his mother made it, but when his father's mother, Grandma Carolina, from Mexico would visit, he was particularly effusive, saying "*Estos si son huevos rancheros ala perfección.*" Roughly translated, that's "these huevos rancheros are perfection." Insert side-eye from Mom.

As it turns out, the main difference was the salsa topping; apparently Grandma Carolina's had the edge. Try it out and see what you think or make adjustments to make it your version of perfección!

1. Make the salsa: In a saucepan over medium heat, roast the tomatoes, chiles, onion, and garlic until browned, about 5 minutes. Transfer the ingredients to a blender; blend until smooth.

2. In a small pot, heat the oil over medium heat; add the blended salsa and salt to taste. Bring to a boil and cook for 5 minutes. Remove from the heat and set aside.

3. In a saucepan over medium heat, heat 2 tablespoons (30 ml) of oil. Once hot, cook the tortillas until golden on both sides, about 15 seconds per side. Set aside.

4. Make the eggs: Put 1 tablespoon (15 ml) of the oil in the pan and heat over medium-high heat. Once the oil is hot, crack the eggs and add them to the pan sunny-side up; cook until the

edges are golden, about 3 minutes. Remove from the heat and
set aside.

5. In a medium-size pot over medium heat, cook the refried beans
   with the remaining tablespoon (15 ml) of oil until warm, about
   5 minutes.

6. To serve, place two tortillas on each plate; top with a cooked
   egg, and cover with salsa. Serve with refried beans and
   tortilla chips.

TJP
(TJ PERKINS)

 RIVERSIDE, CA • **AUGUST 1998**

THE TYPICAL PATH for an American to become a star luchador in Mexico is to first become a star in the US—but not much has been typical about the career of TJ Perkins. From a young age, TJ knew he wanted to be a pro wrestler, but he assumed that he'd have to graduate high school first and figured he would wrestle for his high school team and learn skills he could use later. But days into his freshman year in high school, he found out that his school did not even have a team. Rather than deterring the thirteen-year-old, he decided he was going to find a local wrestling school and start on his dream right away.

Most pro wrestling schools will not enroll students under the age of eighteen, but lucky for TJ, he was in Los Angeles, where lucha libre schools are willing to start kids practically from the time they can walk. With one year of training under his belt, TJ debuted at age fourteen, and by the time he was sixteen, he was leaving school early on Fridays to be on the road all weekend as a professional wrestler and getting back to typical high school life come Monday.

Just a few years later, TJ was part of the very first New Japan Dojo class in Los Angeles and, at just seventeen, trained alongside future WWE headliners Bryan Danielson, Shinsuke Nakamura, Samoa Joe, and other next-generation top stars. The minute he turned eighteen, New Japan Pro-Wresting (NJPW) gave him a visa and a contract and he was over in Japan wrestling in the country's most famous venue—the Tokyo Dome.

NJPW has had a long-standing relationship with CMLL, the oldest and, many would argue, most respected lucha libre company in Mexico. The two companies had a cross-country talent exchange training program whereby luchadores would head to Japan to train and Japanese wrestlers would move to Mexico for a period of time to train. At eighteen, TJ had gone from the US to Japan and now to Mexico. At the end of 2003, he would win two major CMLL fan voted awards: Best New Sensation (essentially Rookie of the Year) and Feud of the Year, which was for a trios feud of TJ, Rocky Romero, and Ricky Reyes (collectively Los Havana Brothers) vs. Volador Jr., Virus, and Ricky Marvin.

At an age at which most pro wrestlers have barely

even started their training, TJP had become a lucha libre sensation. For the next thirteen years, TJ would compete in nearly every major promotion, and dozens of smaller ones, throughout the world, including IMPACT Wrestling, Ring of Honor, Pro Wrestling Guerrilla, and even the pilot episode of MTV's *Wrestling Society X*. He would win tournaments and championships from coast to coast. And, when opportunity allowed, he would return to his lucha libre roots, be it wrestling for a Masked Republic pay-per-view event or joining the cast of Lucha VaVOOM as the masked firefighter El Bombero.

In 2016, the WWE decided to bring a focus back to the heavily lucha libre–influenced cruiserweight style of wrestling. WWE recruited a number of top prospects from around the globe and held the first Cruiserweight Classic tournament where the winner would become the very first WWE Cruiserweight Champion of the modern era. With eighteen years of experience under his belt and a graduate level education in every style of wrestling on the planet, TJ entered the tournament, and after defeating top talents from Germany, the US, Japan, and Mexico, he was crowned winner and champion.

TJ would remain competing in WWE for the next three years. Then, in 2019, he asked for his release from the company so that he could venture out on his own again as an independent and make his way back to the company that first believed in him, NJPW. The wrestling scene in 2020 was much different than it was in any era leading up to it. And, for TJP, that meant being part of three major brands—NJPW, IMPACT Wrestling, and Major League Wrestling. And, thanks to the alliance between IMPACT Wrestling and Lucha Libre AAA, TJ has even spent time back in Mexico wrestling many of the great cruiserweight talents in the country where he first became a sensation.

Although most sports would see an athlete heading into retirement after twenty-two years, this is rarely the case with lucha libre, where stars, such as one of TJ's trainers while in CMLL, Negro Casas (see his family story and nephew Tiger's recipe on page 289), have been wrestling for more than forty years with no end in sight. The question isn't if TJP will continue to bring his hybrid style to the ring; rather, it is where will the superstar end up next?

FUN FACTS

* TJP has worn nine different masks throughout his career before he ever stepped foot into the WWE as himself and became the first WWE Cruiserweight Champion of the modern era.

* Not a typical career, not a typical pet: TJP has two pet pigs, Pugsley and Cupcake.

* TJP has become a source of pride for Filipinos in both the US and the Philippines, where his WWE run garnered him superstar status. The Fil-Am Flash is very proud of his cultural heritage and one of his 25+ tattoos is the Filipino "sun and three stars." He's also got a lot of really cool lucha-related ones.

LONGGANISA AND FRIED RICE

SERVES
2
(on 1 really hungry luchador)

1½ to 2 pounds (680 to 905 g) longganisa sausage

3 to 4 tablespoons (45 to 60 ml) olive or vegetable oil, plus more if needed

3 garlic cloves, minced

2 cups (390 g) uncooked rice, cooked

Salt and freshly ground black pepper

Parsley flakes or finely chopped green onions, for garnish

Sausage lovers are gonna love this recipe for *longganisa* and fried rice. Longganisa is the Filipino cousin of longaniza, a chorizo-esque Spanish sausage. It's typically served alongside fried rice as a breakfast dish in the Philippines, and it's a personal favorite of TJ Perkins.

Perkins has traveled the world as a luchador since the age of eighteen, so he's often a long way from home—and from the comfort of this favorite dish. Happily, his mother gave him the recipe, which allows him to re-create a taste of home no matter where in the world he may be.

1. In a saucepan, heat the longganisa and ½ cup (120 ml) of water over medium-high heat for about 3 minutes, until the water evaporates, then cook for 15 to 20 minutes more, or until the internal temperature reaches about 160°F (about 71°C).

2. Meanwhile, in a separate saucepan, heat the oil over high heat. Add the garlic and cook until golden brown, about 1 minute.

3. Add the rice; if needed, add 1 to 2 tablespoons (15 to 30 ml) of water. Cook until warm and fragrant, adding salt and pepper to taste and more water, if needed.

4. When the rice is cooked to your liking, stir in the parsley and mix briefly. Remove from the heat and serve with the sausage.

LOS BRAZOS
New Generation

FROM **MEXICO CITY, MEXICO**

BRAZO DE ORO JR.: **SEPTEMBER 2013**

BRAZO CIBERNÉTICO JR.: **AUGUST 2009**

BRAZO CELESTIAL: **OCTOBER 2010**

THE ALVARADO FAMILY is one of the largest and oldest families in lucha libre. The patriarch of the family, Juan Alvarado Ibarra, started wrestling in the 1940s under the name Shadito Cruz and wrestled for decades. Juan and his wife, Ana Nieves, had six sons, all of whom became luchadores, the famous trios Los Brazos: El Brazo, Brazo de Oro, Brazo de Plata (aka Super Porky), and Brazo de Platino, Súper Brazo, and Brazo Cibernético (aka Robin Hood).

Los Brazos was one of the original trios teams during a period in the early 1980s when trios matches became extremely popular. Brazos was well known for their battles with such teams as Los Villanos and Los Infernales, including the famous October 21, 1988, trios apuestas match at Plaza de Toros en Monumental in Monterrey. Brazos put up their three masks against the masks of Villanos I, IV, and V and ended up losing the match in front of a sold-out bullring, as more than fifteen thousand fans looked on.

The next generation in the Alvarado family grew even larger. It includes La Máscara, Maximo, Psycho Clown, Goya Kong, Robin, Aramís, Arquero, Alimaña, Muñeca de Plata, El Hijo del Brazo de Platino, Brazo de Oro Jr., Brazo Cibernético Jr., Brazo Celestial, and possibly more.

Their family extends even further when you take marriages into account. For example, Goya Kong is married to Carta Brava Jr.; India Sioux is the wife of Máximo, which extends to the large lucha family of Pirata Morgan, who is Sioux's uncle. Dozens and dozens of luchadores and luchadoras who are part of one very large, and strong, family tree!

BRAZOS FAMILY MEMBER *PSYCHO CLOWN*

Brazo de Oro Jr. is the son of Brazo de Oro. Brazo Cibernético Jr. is the son of Robin Hood, who also wrestled under the name Brazo Cibernético. His brother competes under the name Robin. Brazo Celestial has also wrestled under the name Súper Brazo Jr. and is the son of Súper Brazo. Many members of the Alvarado family work in the offices of the major lucha libre promotions and, as the family grows, continue to show the influence and importance the Brazos have had on lucha libre.

LA MÁSCARA

MAXIMO

LEFT TO RIGHT: BRAZO DE ORO JR, BRAZO CELESTIAL

MEXICAN BEEF STEAK

SERVES
4 to 6

BEEF STEAK:

1 medium-size white onion,
  chopped (about 1 cup [160 g])

2¼ pounds (1 kg) sirloin steak

2 teaspoons (11 g) garlic salt

2 medium-size fresh jalapeño
  peppers, chopped

4 medium-size tomatoes, diced

¼ cup (60 ml) vegetable oil

GUACAMOLE:

3 medium-size tomatillos

2 fresh jalapeño peppers

1 garlic clove

½ medium-size white onion

5 ripe avocados, peeled, pitted,
  and mashed

1 teaspoon (6 g) kosher salt, or
  to taste

Serving Suggestion

Serve portions of steak with a generous scoop of guacamole.

Mexican beef steak is a beloved comfort food classic in many a Mexican household, luchador homes included! The busy lucha libre lifestyle doesn't allow a ton of time for cooking complicated meals, so this is a popular and satisfying favorite in the Alvarado abode, home of "The Bad Boys" Brazo de Oro Jr., Brazo Cibernético Jr., and Brazo Celestial.

Rich, flavorful steak served with guacamole and refried beans is like eating a warm hug. As a bonus, it comes together quickly enough to allow for a meal with family or friends even when time is tight.

1. Make the beef steak: In a saucepan, fry the chopped onion over medium heat for 2 to 3 minutes, or until it is golden and translucent. Remove the onion from the pan, retaining the liquid.

2. In the same pan, in the residual liquid, sprinkle the sirloin with the garlic salt and cook for 10 minutes over medium-low heat. Once cooked, remove the meat, reserving the liquid.

3. In the same pan, in the residual liquid, cook the chopped jalapeños for 3 minutes. Add the tomatoes and cook for 3 additional minutes.

4. Add the reserved onion and meat, cover the pot, and cook over low heat for 10 minutes.

5. Make the guacamole: In a food processor or blender, liquefy the tomatillos, jalapeños, garlic, and onion.

6. Transfer the mixture to a large bowl.

7. Add the mashed avocado. Stir to combine, adding salt.

MINI REY MISTERIO
(Octagóncito II)

 MARTINEZ DE LA TORRE, VERACRUZ, MEXICO ◆ **DECEMBER 1995**

ONE OF THE many, many things Lucha Libre AAA founder Antonio Peña is credited for is turning the Mini-Estrellas division into a legitimate draw in lucha libre. A "mini" is a luchador who is smaller in size than a typical performer. Although, oftentimes, minis have biological factors, such as dwarfism, others are simply short, often 5 feet tall or less. The shortest minis have been around 3 foot 7 (109 cm). Peña's first megastars of the minis division were Mascarita Sagrada and the original Octagóncito (who would go on to have many different names later). Just as important, however,

was Octagóncito II, who took over the persona in 1997 after the original left AAA for Promo Azteca in 1996.

One of the most talented Mini-Estrellas in history, Octagóncito II enjoyed a decade-long run with the promotion before leaving in 2017. The lucha star would then strike a deal with Rey Misterio Sr. for the rights to become the "mini" of the famed luchador, lucha trainer, and uncle to WWE superstar Rey Mysterio, and he became Mini Rey Misterio. The legendary Mini-Estrella continues to be a top luchador on the indie circuit, still flying as high as ever even into his forties.

FUN FACTS

* Octagóncito II was also the second La Parkita in addition to being Mini Rey Misterio, making him one of the few luchadores to portray three different Mini-Estrella versions of famous luchadores.
* He has had three major championship reigns,

having held the AAA World Mini-Estrellas Championship once and the Mexican National Mini's Championship twice.
* Keeping lucha libre in the family, he is married to luchadora Lady Sensación.

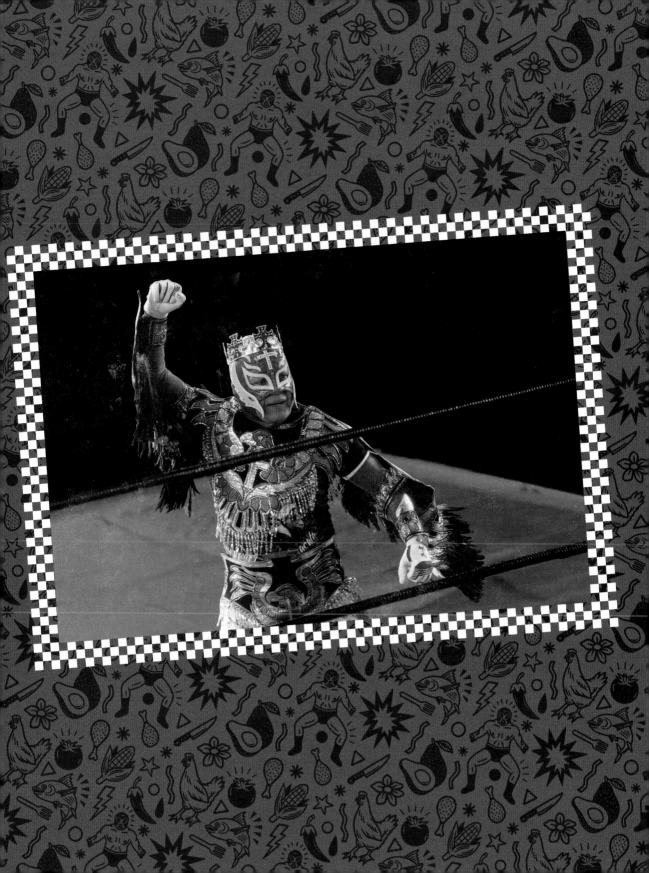

MEXICAN CHICKEN BREASTS WITH SALAD

SERVES
1

2 tablespoons (30 ml) extra-virgin olive oil

½ medium-size white onion, sliced

3 serrano peppers, seeded and chopped

½ large chicken breast, cut into strips

Salt and freshly ground black pepper

½ medium-size tomato, chopped

TO SERVE (QUANTITIES TO TASTE):

Lettuce

Sliced cucumber

Avocado

Salt

Extra-virgin olive oil

Tortillas

Good things come in small packages—few know this better than Mini Rey Misterio, one of the greatest luchador "minis" of all time. In contrast to standard luchadores, a mini luchador requires a greater degree of agility, elasticity, and speed. That means plenty of preparation and training are required to remain in peak physical condition.

The right diet matters too. Feel-good food that tastes delicious and helps provide clean, powerful energy is the name of the game. This easy recipe for Mexican chicken breasts with salad is healthy, nourishing, and bound to become your new go-to weekday dinner.

1. In a saucepan, heat the oil over medium-high heat for about 3 minutes, or until it shimmers. Once hot, add the onion; sauté until it turns golden and translucent.

2. Add the serrano peppers and let the mixture cook for about 5 minutes, stirring frequently.

3. Add the chicken breast and cover the pan. Cook, stirring every 5 minutes, for 8 to 10 minutes, or until the chicken is cooked through; add salt and pepper to taste.

4. Add the tomato, stir to incorporate, and cover the pan again.

5. Prepare your plate: Assemble a handful of lettuce, cucumber, avocado, salt, and oil to taste, then top with the chicken mixture. Serve tortillas on the side.

PREP: CHOP VEGGIES.

GOOD
THINGS
COME
in
small packages!

JOE BARKER

 WAKEFIELD, WEST YORKSHIRE, ENGLAND

HE'S A BRIT known best by his online name Meetloaf, so one may not expect him to be arguably the biggest lucha libre fan in the UK, and possibly all of Europe. But he certainly can make that claim.

The cohost of the luchacentric podcast *The MMMShow* (Masks, Mats & Mayhem) on the Lucha Central Podcast Network resides in Falmouth, a southern city of England, some 300 miles (483 km) from London and that city's fairly strong local lucha scene. Joe's love of wrestling began sometime around 1997, when his mother would watch *WCW Nitro* and he quickly found himself enthralled with the cruiserweight division. His favorites at the time were Último Dragón, Eddie Guerrero, Rey Misterio Jr., Psychosis, La Parka, and Juventud Guerrera (see Guerrera's recipe for Cochinita Pibil on page 114).

Like many wrestling fans, once the WWE purchased WCW in 2001, Joe's interest started to wane until eventually he became a "lapsed fan." This is where Joe found himself from the mid-2000s until about ten years later in January 2015, when a friend told him that he had to watch a new TV series called *Lucha Underground*.

That show hooked Joe back into wrestling and well past his original fandom. This would open an opportunity to join the *Lucha Underground*–centric *Masks, Mats & Mayhem* podcast as a cohost. The next thing he knew, he was talking to luchadores and TV series producers. The supermarket worker who loved lucha libre at ten years old but lived more than 5,000 miles from Mexico City was now in the thick of things. As the *Lucha Underground* stars began to appear on wrestling events in England, Joe began to venture out from his southern town more and more. He drove 1,100 miles (1,770 km) to meet Penta Zero M (page 94) for the first time. That fateful day would also mark the beginning of Joe's authentic lucha libre mask collection. The now museum quality collection also boasts ring-worn pieces from Penta's brother Rey Fenix (see page 174) and likely the world's largest collection of El Hijo del Fantasma (now Santos Escobar in WWE) masks and gear.

And, while Joe may be envious of others' abilities to get to lucha libre shows in an easier manner, it's safe to say that many of those fans are envious of Joe's insane authentic mask and memorabilia collection, likely the largest in all of Europe.

MEXICAN SHEPHERD'S PIE

SERVES
6

5 Maris Piper potatoes, peeled and quartered (see notes)

1½ tablespoons (21 g) unsalted butter

Salt and freshly ground black pepper

17.5 ounces (500 g) ground lamb

1 medium-size white onion (about ½ cup [80 g]), chopped

3 garlic cloves, finely chopped

3 tablespoons (20 g) taco seasoning

6.75 ounces (200 ml) lamb stock

1 (14-ounce [400 g]) can chopped tomatoes

Splash of Worcestershire sauce

Fresh chile peppers (optional)

1 (14-ounce [400 g]) can kidney beans, drained and rinsed

2 cups (240 g) grated cheese of your choosing

When you think of fusion food, Mexican-meets-British creations probably aren't the first things that come to mind. However, this dish proves it's not only possible, but the results are universally (or at least globally) delicious.

Joe "Pepe" Barker is not only recognized as the UK's biggest lucha libre fan, but he's also very creative in the kitchen. He dreamed up this dish to make English cooking more palatable to his partner, Paula. The resulting pie, like him, is English in design, but its heart has been touched by Mexico.

NOTES: Chiles can be hard to come by in England, so this recipe doesn't include a ton of spice. If you're a heat seeker, feel free to augment!

Barker favors Maris Piper potatoes for their creamy texture, but if you're unable to find them, Yukon Gold potatoes will work just fine.

1. Fill a large, deep pot with 8½ cups (2 L) of water. Bring to a boil. Add the potatoes and boil until tender; a sharp knife should slide easily into the potatoes with little resistance.

2. Drain water from the pot, keep the potatoes in it for mashing.

3. Add the butter plus salt and pepper to taste.

4. Mash thoroughly, making sure to get rid of all lumps. Nobody likes lumpy mash!

5. In a large, deep skillet, heat the ground lamb over medium-high heat for 5 minutes. Once browned on the first side, flip and cook the second side for another 5 minutes. Once browned, transfer the lamb to a dish and set aside. Drain most of the fat from the pan (a little residual fat will help during the next step).

6. In the same pan, in the residual lamb fat, fry the onion over medium heat until browned and softened, 5 to 10 minutes.

7. Add garlic, fry for another minute or two, until browned.

8. Return the lamb to the pan and mix well.

9. Add the taco seasoning and fry for 1 minute, before adding the lamb stock, tomatoes, Worcestershire sauce, and your desired quantity of chiles, if using.

10. Bring the mixture to a boil, then lower the heat and simmer until the liquid has thickened and clings to the meat. Add the kidney beans and cook until they are warmed, 5 to 10 minutes.

11. Meanwhile, position a rack in the middle of the oven and preheat the oven to 350°F (180 C).

12. Spoon the filling into an 11 x 17-inch (28 x 43 cm) casserole dish. Spread evenly and top with about half the grated cheese.

13. Carefully spoon the mashed potatoes on top of the filling. Use the tines of a fork to create lines about ½ inch (1.3 cm) deep before sprinkling the rest of the cheese on top.

14. Bake, uncovered, for 15 minutes, or until golden brown. To achieve a nice crispy top, put under a hot grill or broiler for a couple of minutes toward the end of the baking time, but be careful not to burn it.

REY FENIX

 MEXICO CITY, MEXICO ◆ **APRIL 2005**

TO SAY REY Fenix is completely different from his brother and tag team partner Penta Zero M would be an insult to the term *understatement*. Whereas Penta Zero M is a brawler and a half, Rey Fenix prefers to come at opponents with the traditional high-flying lucha libre style. That's a good thing because no one does this style better than Rey Fenix, who is not only the premier high flyer in wrestling but also a talent who seems to pull out new moves and new ideas every single time he's in the ring. And while he's better known as a tag wrestler these days, Rey Fenix has had plenty of success as a singles luchador, with reigns as Lucha Libre AAA Mega Champion and Lucha Underground Champion, the latter title making him and Penta Zero M the only brother combo to hold that title.

FUN FACTS

* Rey Fenix has also wrestled under the names Máscara Oriental, Fenix, Fenix El Rey, and King Phoenix; the latter name he used when he wrestled for Consejo Mundial de Lucha Libre (CMLL).
* Along with current WWE star Ricochet, he's the only luchador in Lucha Underground history to have held all three titles in the promotion (the Lucha Underground Championship, Gift of the Gods Championship, and Lucha Underground Trios Championships).
* Like his brother, Rey Fenix has his own catchphrase: "*Animo!*" (Let's go!).

MEXAKING WRAP

SERVES

1

1 lime, cut in half

8 ounces (about 225 g) boneless, skinless chicken breast, cut into ¼-inch (6 mm) strips

8 ounces (225 g) skirt steak, cut into ¼-inch (6 mm) strips

Cooking spray, for pan

3 slices turkey bacon

2 medium-size nopales tortillas

2 tablespoons (5 g) chopped fresh cilantro

Salsa, for serving

Luchadores are athletes so eating well is important, yet the traveling lifestyle required for the sport can make it challenging to maintain a healthy eating regimen. Rey Fenix doesn't always get to take time for a multicourse meal, but this quick, protein-packed wrap gives him plenty of satisfying flavor and nutrition that he can enjoy on the go.

The MexaKing Wrap is simple yet satisfying, combining various types of meat served in low-carb *nopales* tortillas. If you like the idea of this wrap but prefer a different filling, try it out with Penta Zero M's (Rey Fenix's Lucha Brothers partner and real-life brother) chicken fajitas recipe on page 97 or Jerry Villagrana's carne asada or pollo asado recipes on pages 84 and 204.

1. Squeeze the juice from one lime half over the chicken and steak. Reserve the second lime half.
2. Spray a large, nonstick pan with cooking spray. Add the chicken, steak, and turkey bacon. Cook until done: the chicken should have an internal temperature of about 165°F (73°C), the steak should have an internal temperature of about 145°F (63°C) if you prefer it medium or 160° to 165°F (71° to 73°C) for well done, and the turkey bacon should be crisped to your liking.
3. Once cooled, slice the meat into small cubes or pieces.
4. In a skillet over high heat, briefly heat the tortillas, removing them when they become golden (it will take only a few seconds).

RECIPE CONTINUED >

CHECK PAGE 94 for Penta Zero M's story

STEP SEVEN: SPRINKLE CILANTRO.

5. To assemble, layer the two tortillas so that about one-quarter of them overlap—the idea is to create one extra-long tortilla.

6. Place the meat in the center along the entire length of the tortilla, with a small portion uncovered on each end.

7. Sprinkle the cilantro on top of the meat. Squeeze the juice of the second lime half on top.

8. Roll from the edge nearest you, folding in the sides as you roll to create a burrito-like seal. Serve with salsa on the side.

What are nopales tortillas?

Also called cactus tortillas, these tortillas are made with mashed cactus in addition to traditional corn flour. They're lower in carbs than traditional tortillas, making them a favorite among health-conscious luchadores! If you're unable to locate nopales tortillas, traditional tortillas will work just fine.

See pages 94–97 for Penta Zero M's story and Chicken Fajitas with Bell Peppers.

CENTVRIÓN

 MEXICO CITY, MEXICO ◆ **FEBRUARY 2008**

TRAINED IN PART by the legendary indie luchador Black Terry, Centvrión spent the bulk of his early career as a high-flying sensation in the International Wrestling Revolution Group, teaming with the likes of Dinamic Black and current AAA star Golden Magic to battle indie stars Alan Extreme, current AAA star Carta Brava Jr., Imposible, Látigo, and even his former trainer Terry. Still on the indies and having killer matches, Centvrión is young enough that it's not out of the realm of possibility that you'll see him in the big leagues one of these days.

FUN FACTS

* Centvrión is a former IWC Light Heavyweight Champion.
* He was a member of the trios team La Mala Hierba (The Bad Weed), with fellow indie stars Fly Warrior and Látigo.

* The name Centvrión comes from the word *centurion*, an ancient Roman commander, the original inspiration for his persona.

PAREJAS DE TAMALES
(TAG TEAM TAMALES), SWEET AND SAVORY

MAKES
about 20
tamales

20 to 30 corn husks

8.8 ounces (250 g) lard

1 tablespoon (14 g) baking soda

1 tablespoon (14 g) baking powder

1 tablespoon (18 g) kosher salt

2¼ pounds (1 kg) tamale flour

¾ cup (150 g) sugar

3 drops of red vegetable coloring

6⅓ cups (1.5 L) chicken stock

FOR ASSEMBLY:

21 ounces (600 g) chicken breast, cooked

17 ounces (500 ml) prepared red mole

21 ounces (600 g) pork leg, cooked

17 ounces (about 500 ml) salsa verde

Did you know that tamales date back to as early as 8000 BC? They're said to have been favored in Aztec and Mayan times as an easily transportable food for hunting trips and traveling.

Tamales are just as delicious today, but making them is somewhat arduous, so they're typically reserved for special occasions when a big batch is in order. For Centvrión and his family, tamales are synonymous with holidays: "In my family, tamales are relegated most often at the end of the year. No matter what we dine on those dates, tamales can never be missing."

This recipe is based on his mother's—they suggest enjoying them with *atole*, a delicious Mexican hot chocolate drink.

1. Prepare the corn leaves/husks in advance by soaking them in warm water for 1 hour and then in cold water overnight.

2. Make the tamale filling: In a medium-size bowl, using a mixer or by hand, beat the lard with 5 ice cubes. The lard is added with the ice and beaten until white and fluffy—by then the ice cubes should melt; if not, the small pieces left can be removed.

3. Add the baking soda, baking powder, and salt. Continue to beat for 3 minutes.

4. Transfer the mixture to a large bowl and combine with tamale flour.

5. Remove one-quarter of the mixture; transfer to a separate bowl for making sweet tamales. Add the sugar and food coloring to the smaller portion to make red mole.

6. Add the chicken stock to the larger portion and knead. With a baking spatula, take the bottom mix to the top and so on in circles for 20 minutes. It is important that the rhythm and constancy of kneading be maintained in both mixtures, so it's good to have a friend help you with one of the batches.

7. To test whether the dough is ready, drop a small portion into a glass of water. If it's ready, it should float immediately. The consistency should be malleable and spreadable so that it won't spill onto the steamer sheet. If required, continue to knead.

SWEET TAMALES:

1. Place a generous amount of the red mixture on the soaked corn husks and wrap.

SAVORY TAMALES:

1. For chicken tamales, place a portion of chicken and 2 tablespoons (31 g) of red mixture on the husk before placing the dough mixture on top and wrapping.

2. For pork tamales, place a portion of pork leg and 2 tablespoons (32 g) of salsa verde on the husk before placing the dough mixture on top and wrapping.

COOKING THE TAMALES:

1. Place the wrapped corn husks in a steamer, aligning them vertically to accommodate as many as possible. Steam for 1 to 2½ hours (it may take longer if the tamales are in two layers), or when the tamales have detached completely from the husks. To test doneness, pull one from the center of the steamer and see whether it separates easily from the husk. If so, the whole batch should be done.

DEMUS

 SALTILLO, COAHUILA, MEXICO • **JUNE 1997**

DEMUS GREW UP as a fan of lucha libre, eventually leading him to the hallowed halls of the *gimnasio* in Tijuana where he was trained by Rey Misterio Sr., along with Psychosis and his brother Fobia. Being on the smaller side when he debuted, Demus was quickly moved to the Mini-Estrella division for Consejo Mundial de Lucha Libre. Working for CMLL, he took the name Pequeño Damián 666 after the full-size luchador Damian 666. And, like the larger-size Damian, Pequeño Damián took on a tag team partner, Pequeño Halloween, and they formed their own version of Perros del Mal called Los Perritos del Mal.

In 2010, Pequeño Damián underwent a name change to Demus 3:16 (a play on both the name being close to 333, which is half of 666, and on the famous "Stone Cold" Steve Austin 3:16 saying familiar to pro wrestling fans worldwide: "You can talk about your Psalms. You can talk about your John 3:16. Austin 3:16 says I just whipped your ass," which led to wrestling fans around the globe purchasing Austin 3:16 tees and the kickoff of the wrestling boom of the 1990s). As one of the larger Mini-Estrellas, Demus (he is 5 foot 3 [160 cm], whereas fellow mini-star Mascarita Dorada is a whole 10 inches [25.5 cm] shorter at 4 foot 5 [134.6 cm]), was given an opportunity to advance to compete with full-size luchadores at CMLL's eighteenth anniversary of Mini-Estrellas as part of two *torneo cibernético* matches. On August 24 of that year, Demus 3:16 defeated Pierrothito in the finals to move up to the heavyweight/full-size wrestler division. In 2011, however, he would lose an apuestas match to Virus and was forced to not only lose his hair but to return to the mini's division.

In 2017 he would leave CMLL and drop "3:16" from his name and furthermore be known as Demus El Demonio, or simply Demus for short. Today, Demus has become a regular in Lucha Libre AAA as well as being featured on independent events throughout Mexico and the US. He is locked into a new war with Mascarita Dorada, which has carried over into many promotions and countries, as these two make magic when they are on opposite sides of each other in a ring.

Like many luchadores, the sport is a family affair. Demus's father and brother are luchadores and he even married a luchadora named Hiroka, gaining two brothers-in-law who are also luchadores.

PASTA WITH MUSHROOMS

SERVES
4

5 tablespoons (75 ml) extra-virgin olive oil

7 ounces (200 g) spaghetti or fettuccine

2 tablespoons (28 g) unsalted butter

1 garlic clove, finely chopped

8 to 9 ounces (225 to 255 g) white or cremini mushrooms, sliced into quarters, stems discarded

2¼ cups (518 g) sour cream

8 to 9 ounces (225 to 255 g) Mexican Manchego cheese, for garnish

Salt and freshly ground black pepper

For Demus, despite his "stay back!" appearance, being a luchador is never lonely. For him, the sport is a family affair; his fathers and brothers are luchadores. But wait, there's more: he also married a luchadora and his two brothers-in-law are luchadores as well—always plenty to talk about over family dinners.

This recipe is one of the family's favorite main dishes, featuring pasta served in a rich, creamy, and earthy mushroom sauce. Whether you're a family of luchadores or just love watching the sport, this cozy and comforting recipe is ideal for cooler-weather months.

1. Fill a large pot with 4¼ cups (1 L) of water, 3 tablespoons (45 ml) of the oil, and a pinch of salt. Bring to a boil.

2. Add the pasta and boil for 10 minutes. Drain and rinse with cold water. Add 1 tablespoon (15 ml) of the olive oil to prevent sticking; set aside.

3. In a large saucepan, melt the butter over medium heat. Add the garlic; cook for about 30 seconds, then add the mushrooms. Cook until lightly browned, about 3 minutes.

4. Lower the heat to low. Add the pasta and sour cream; cook for 20 minutes.

5. To serve, garnish portions with Mexican Manchego cheese and salt and pepper to taste.

DOS HERMANOS LUCHA

(Corey and Jimmy Kane)

COREY KANE:

 PITTSBURGH, PA

JIMMY KANE:

 PITTSBURGH, PA

WHEN MOST PEOPLE in central Pennsylvania think of forms of entertainment, lucha libre doesn't exactly top the list. The Friday-night lights and hunting trips often overshadow the squared circle. However, such is not the case for two brothers who now commonly refer to themselves as Dos Hermanos Lucha.

Pennsylvania native brothers Jimmy and Corey grew up with many of the same interests as their peers. Weekends were typically consumed with traditional American sports, but one interest in particular set them apart from others—lucha libre.

As products of the WWF "Attitude Era," the huge wrestling boom of the 1990s where more than twelve million Americans were watching pro wrestling weekly, the brothers became obsessed.

Being glued to the TV for the Monday Night Wars between WWF and WCW was the highlight of their week. When not watching wrestling, the *Do Not Try This at Home* warning videos that preceeded wrestling programming were highly disregarded as the boys organized matches in their backyard.

Although the "main event" talent within both major promotions helped shape the brothers, they, like so many other current-day lucha fans, often credit the first hour of *WCW Nitro*, which would feature luchadores in action, for why they fell in love with the Mexican version of the sport.

"Seeing these guys in masks with the flashy colors and performing acrobatics we had never seen before made them seem like real-life superheroes. The showcasing of a completely different style of wrestling opened our eyes to a world we never knew existed," said Jimmy, the older of the brothers.

In this era before the internet was household technology, the brothers had to find different ways to research the Mexican culture. Younger brother Corey recalls flipping channels on their father's satellite TV and finding lucha libre on Galavisíon in the late '90s. Like so many other fans who had discovered lucha libre through WCW, they had no idea what the Spanish TV commentators were saying. Nonetheless, they enjoyed every minute of it.

From that point on, the brothers idolized and often imitated such stars as Abismo Negro, Máscara Sagrada, Juventud Guerrera (see page 110), Psychosis (see page 222), Último Dragón, La Parka, and Rey Misterio Jr. And, while other interests and trends in their lives have come and gone over the past twenty years, their love of lucha libre has remained a constant.

Modern advancements in technology have allowed not only for fans to stay in the know about lucha libre much better, but bilingual websites, such as LuchaCentral.com, deliver daily news and videos of lucha goings-on in Mexico and updates on the luchadores in WWE and other major companies around the globe. With more luchadores coming to perform in the US and with such social media platforms as Facebook, Twitter, and Instagram giving fans direct access to the stars, it has led to a rapid expansion of the brothers' expression of their lucha passion—building one of the world's greatest lucha libre mask collections.

The brothers often explain to others when asked that they have always been collectors of something throughout their lives. From baseball cards to comics to sports and movie memorabilia, they have always been intrigued by hunting and owning rare pieces.

"Collecting lucha libre memorabilia in particular allows us to get closer than we ever thought we could," said Jimmy. "In its purest form, it is quite frankly history preservation of art." Many pieces in the DH Lucha collection have a memory or story attached. Whether it's a connection to a trip the brothers made together to personally witness the mask worn in a match or it was worn in a bout that is a highlight in a luchador's career, they feel it is very important to preserve that history and share it with others.

Their collection currently includes around one hundred luchada (fought-in/ring-worn) masks, among many other pieces of lucha libre ring attire. Unlike many other collectors who focus on the vintage masks of the 1950s through '70s, Dos Hermanos Lucha prefer to focus on masks of the era they have actually been watching from the mid-'90s to today. Their collection has become so impressive that lucha libre convention Expo Lucha has asked the brothers to begin to exhibit a portion of their collection every year.

PASTOR STUFFED PINEAPPLE

SERVES
4

1¾ pounds (750 g) pork (leg/shoulder), cut into ½-inch (1.3 cm) cubes

10 guajillo chiles

1 garlic clove

2 tablespoons (36 g) salt

½ (3.5-ounce [100 g]) package achiote (annatto paste)

2¼ cups (532 ml) freshly squeezed orange juice

¼ cup (60 ml) white vinegar

1 pineapple

1 ripe avocado, peeled and pitted, cut into ½-inch (1.3 cm) cubes

2 serrano peppers, chopped into tiny cubes (brunoise)

Juice of 1 lime

3 tablespoons (45 ml) vegetable oil

2 medium-size white onions, thinly sliced

For Dos Hermanos Lucha, one of the best things about traveling and visiting new places is the ability to try regional foods that they might not have otherwise been exposed to. So, when they hit a new city, they try to find the best Mexican cuisine the area has to offer.

One of their all-time favorites is *tacos al pastor*. While growing up, they weren't exposed to much beyond beef tacos, so you can imagine the eye-opening experience of al pastor—a rich pork– and pineapple–flavored combination—that for them remains a game changer.

1. Wash and pat dry the meat. Set aside.
2. Prepare the marinade: Combine the guajillo chiles, garlic, and salt in a large saucepan over medium-high heat. Add 3 cups (710 ml) of water, plus enough to cover the ingredients, if necessary; bring the mixture to a boil, and boil for 20 minutes. Let cool.
3. Transfer the mixture to a blender. Add the achiote, orange juice, and vinegar. Blend until smooth, then strain into a large bowl.
4. Add the meat to the bowl. Cover and refrigerate for 30 minutes.
5. Meanwhile, prepare the pineapple: Cut in half; hollow each half, retaining them as "bowls" for later. Cut the fruit from the hollowed halves into ½-inch (1.3 cm) squares. Set aside.

6. Make the guacamole: In a bowl, combine the avocado, serrano peppers, and lime juice (the lime juice keeps it from browning and adds a nice citrus flavor). Add salt to taste.

7. Cook the meat: In a saucepan, heat the oil over medium heat. Add the onions; cook until soft, about 3 minutes. Lower the heat to low. Add the marinated meat (discard any leftover marinade) and diced pineapple and cook for 30 minutes.

8. To serve, place each pineapple half on a dish. Fill with the cooked pastor meat and serve with guacamole.

What is brunoise?

This French term might sound fancy, but it's actually a pretty simple method of cutting an ingredient. First, you julienne the ingredient, then you give it a quarter turn and dice it again, making tiny, approximately $\frac{1}{8}$-inch (3 mm) cubes. That's it!

EL MIMO AND TROMBA

 MEXICO CITY, MEXICO

EL MIMO: **AUGUST 1998**

TROMBA: **DECEMBER 2013**

EL MIMO AND Tromba are luchadores bound together by blood—a father-and-son duo.

Unlike many of the luchadores in this book who were born into lucha libre, El Mimo discovered the sport later in life. The man of multiple talents first trained as a physical therapist, dancer, and actor. It was as an actor starting to take on more action roles that he felt he had to find a way to learn more agile movements. And so he decided he wanted to study and train in lucha libre.

The art of lucha libre, with everything that surrounds it, was more than enough to make El Mimo fall in love and it was from that point on that he decided to take lucha libre not only as an exercise but also as a profession.

A single father of a one-year-old at the time, El Mimo had no choice but to take his son to training—diaper bag and all. But by the time Tromba would have been old enough to remember the lucha gym, his father was no longer taking him. Because the sport has traditionally worked very hard to protect identities, even from family members, growing up, Tromba did not know that his father was a luchador.

Even when his uncles took him to the lucha libre shows and he saw El Mimo in the ring, he had no idea that the luchador he admired was his own father. One day, the future Tromba was called back to the dressing room area by El Mimo and he revealed who he really was. It was a life-altering experience—his superhero was real, and it was his father!

At that moment, Tromba knew he wanted to follow his footsteps in both careers. Currently, he is studying to become a physical education teacher, in addition to acting in some productions, and of course, wrestling.

PECHUGAS RELLENAS
(STUFFED CHICKEN BREASTS)

SERVES
6

6 boneless, skinless chicken breasts

Freshly ground black pepper

4 ounces (115 g) queso Oaxaca

12 slices turkey ham

Maggi Jugo seasoning sauce, for
dipping chicken

2 tablespoons (30 ml) canola oil,
for frying

SAUCE:

1 (6.7-ounce [190 g]) can
chipotles in adobo sauce

8.5 ounces (250 ml) half-and-half

1 tablespoon canola oil

2 teaspoons (8 g) chicken bouillon
powder

2 teaspoons (12 g) kosher salt

**TO SERVE (OPTIONAL AND
TO TASTE):**

Chopped walnuts

Manchego cheese, cut into small
pieces

Fresh parsley

Talk about keeping it in the family! This recipe for chicken rolled with ham and queso Oaxaca and smothered in a crave-worthy spicy cream sauce comes from father-and-son luchador duo El Mimo and Tromba.

El Mimo is a single father, and as the eldest of four brothers, he had to often pitch in and help around the house . . . and that meant he became masterful at cooking a variety of different dishes (and desserts) for the hungry family.

This dish is a beloved favorite passed on, like the art of being a luchador, from father to son. One taste and you'll easily see why it's so treasured.

1. Sprinkle the chicken breasts with black pepper.
2. Working one breast at a time, sprinkle some queso Oaxaca on top of the breast, then roll with two slices of ham, securing with toothpicks. Repeat with the remaining breasts.
3. Brush the rolls with Maggi Jugo on the exposed side.
4. In a large skillet with a lid, heat the oil over medium heat. Once simmering, fry the breasts, covered, until the chicken has reached an internal temperature of 165°F (73°C).
5. Make the sauce: In a blender, combine the chipotles, 13.5 ounces (400 ml) of water, the half-and-half, canola oil, chicken bouillon powder, and salt. Blend until smooth.

6. Transfer the sauce to a pot and let it come to a boil. Remove from the heat and let cool.
7. When the chicken rolls are fully cooked, dip in the sauce.
8. Serve with a few pieces of chopped walnuts, Manchego cheese, and parsley, for garnish.

DAMIAN 666 AND BESTIA 666

 TIJUANA, BAJA CALIFORNIA, MEXICO

DAMIAN 666: **OCTOBER 1982**

BESTIA 666: **JULY 2009**

AMIAN 666 AND his son, Bestia 666, have terrorized lucha libre rings around the world. Leonardo Carrera Gómez was born June 9, 1961, in Tijuana, Mexico. Damian, as a fan of lucha libre, began training with Luis Canales and the legendary Diablo Velasco. After extensive training under one of the sport's most famed maestros, Leonardo moved back to Tijuana and continued training at Gimnasio de Tijuana under the guidance of Rey Misterio Sr., Miguel López.

Early in his career, Leonardo took on numerous names and personas to varying degrees of success. Caballero 2000 was the name he used when he first debuted in Tijuana, before taking the mantel of Ultraman II (aka Ultraman 2000). Previously, Ultraman had been a major star in Mexico and was a takeoff of the Japanese children's show. His first success came under the mask as Ultraman II, winning the WWA World Trios Championship along with partners KISS and Águilas de América for the Tijuana-based promotion.

In Japan, a promotion called Frontier Martial-Arts Wrestling (FMW) enlisted Leonardo to come and compete for them. Due to trademarks in Japan surrounding the name Ultraman, they gave him the name Amigo Ultra. At the time, FMW was a unique promotion that would feature a crazy hard-core style of wrestling, mixed matches (men and women teaming), and lucha libre. Amigo Ultra, in a costume similar to Ultraman, would often wrestle in straight lucha libre matches on the

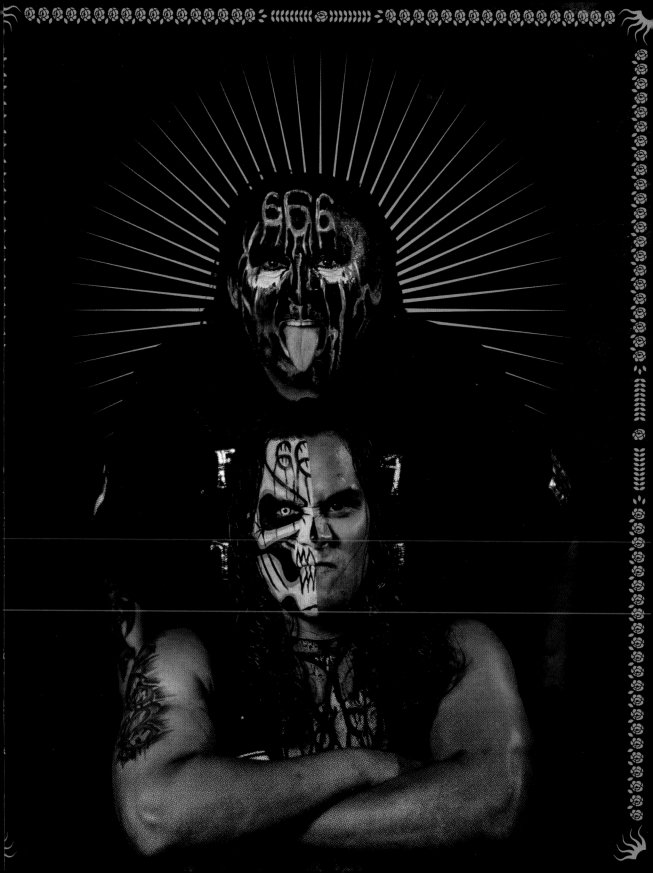

undercard, while his boss, Atsushi Onita, would battle his opponents in matches named "no rope barbed-wire, exploding death matches" and other wild stipulations.

After some time, Onita gave Leonardo a new ring persona. This is where he was given the name Damian. His lucha libre style would become infused with the hard-core style—and a style known to many as "lucha extrema" would grow its roots. Here, Damian developed the hard-core style of wrestling that made him famous. Some of the opponents he encountered while in Japan include Onita himself, the legendary Sheik, his nephew Sabu, and Eiji Ezaki, who would later wrestle as Hayabusa. With his face covered in paint, Damian began painting the numbers 666 onto his forehead, which is when people started calling him Damian 666.

In 1995, Damian 666 represented FMW in the second Stage of the Super J Cup held at Ryogoku Kokugikan in Tokyo, Japan. The Super J Cup is one of wrestling's most prestigious tournaments for cruiserweights and luchadores around the world.

While competing in Japan as Damian 666, he continued to wrestle in Mexico under the name Ultraman 2000. In March 1996, as Ultraman 2000, he lost a mask versus mask match against Psychosis, thus ending his time using the name Ultraman and beginning his time wrestling exclusively as Damian 666.

The year 1996 brought a lot of new experiences for Damian. He was one of the luchadores in a group that Konnan brought to ECW and then later to WCW. For the next four years, Damian wrestled for Ted Turner's World Championship Wrestling and for numerous companies in Mexico. During his time in WCW he would often don a mask and wrestle as Galaxy, pulling double duty on some events. Another memorable moment in WCW took place in 1998, when he joined a stable of luchadores to form the unit called the Latino World Order. Under the watchful eye of their leader Eddie Guerrero, the LWO consisted of La Parka, Hector Garza, Juventud Guerrera, Psychosis, Arturo "Spyder" Flores, and Damian.

After WCW was purchased by the WWE, Damian teamed with frequent partner Ciclope, also known as Halloween. The duo toured Japan with the All Japan Pro Wrestling promotion and worked across the United States and Mexico. On July 20, 2002, Damian and Halloween would win a tournament in Los Angeles to be crowned the first XPW World Tag Team Champions. That same year, the team joined CMLL, the oldest wrestling company in the world. Together along with the former Psychosis, who was now wrestling under the name Nicho el Millonario, the trio formed a unit called La Familia de Tijuana. When Nicho left CMLL, La Familia joined forces with Perro Aguayo Jr.'s group, Los Perros del Mal.

Los Perros del Mal was an amazing group with a rotating cast of luchadores, including Hector Garza, Latin Lover, Mr. Águila, Cibernético, and Damian's son, Bestia 666. In November 2008, the group led by Perro Aguayo Jr. left CMLL and formed their own promotion, Perros del Mal Producciones. Damian continued to wrestle for the company and at the same time worked in the office as the company's main booker helping to bring different talent into the company and to determine what matches would take place.

Damian 666's son, José Leonardo Carrera Lizárraga, began training with his father in Tijuana and under well-respected lucha libre trainer Skayde. Bestia began his career as a luchador competing under the name Leo to gain experience without having to live up to the expectations of being the son of a famous luchador.

When the time was right, José painted his face in a similar fashion as his father and took on the name Bestia 666. In 2009, he started wrestling preliminary matches for Perros del Mal Producciones. A year later, he was part of a group from Los Perros del Mal that "invaded" Lucha Libre AAA. This is where he gained much of his early success as he teamed with his father and his old friend Halloween in trios matches facing the team of Los Psycho Circus, which comprised Psycho Clown, Monster Clown, and Murder Clown. The trio also wrestled across Mexico representing Los Perros del Mal.

Early success continued for Bestia, and on July 24, 2011, Los Perros del Mal created its first ever Light Heavyweight Championship in a six-way match, with Bestia coming out on top.

In the US, lucha libre started becoming more and more popular due to the popularity of Rey Mysterio, the influence of Konnan, and access to matches being more available on YouTube and streaming services. He appeared briefly on the Robert Rodriguez–produced television series *Lucha Underground*, which played a part in increasing the popularity of lucha libre in the US. He's also become a top-tier talent in promotions throughout the US, including PCW Ultra, DEFY, and Wildkat Sports & Entertainment.

For the last number of years, Bestia has called home The Crash lucha libre promotion based out of Tijuana. It is there that he became one-half of The Crash Tag Team Champions with partner Mecha Wolf. During his time competing for The Crash, he has won two lucha de apuestas Hair vs. Hair matches: one against Jack Evans in 2016, and the other against Ángel Garza (now of WWE fame) in 2018.

As independent wrestling and lucha libre soar in popularity, Bestia 666 has earned a spot as one of the industry's hottest commodities.

PEPPER STEAK

MAKES
4
servings

1 cup (80 g) whole peppercorns, ground

4 (1-pound [455 g]) New York strip steaks

¼ cup (½ stick, 55 g) unsalted butter, plus more if needed

2 tablespoons (30 g) extra-virgin olive oil

2 shallots, finely chopped

3 tablespoons (45 ml) brandy or cognac

½ cup (120 ml) red wine

8.5 ounces (251 ml) beef or vegetable stock

½ cup (120 ml) heavy cream

1 teaspoon (4 g) Dijon mustard

Salt and freshly ground black pepper

Flat-leaf parsley, for garnish

As a rule, luchadores love steak. After all, it's a very physical profession, and a high-protein meal like steak can help them eat well and stay in peak physical form.

This recipe is a cut above, featuring buttery steak, wine-infused shallots, and a luscious mustard cream sauce. These restaurant-quality results may have something to do with the fact that lucha legends Damian 666 and his son, Bestia 666, adapted it from the work of Ittoh Rodríguez, a popular Tijuana chef and lucha-beloved nutritionist (who also inspired the recipe for Spanish Tortilla, page 226). But don't worry: It's actually easy to prepare! Whether you're terrorizing opponents in the ring like the 666 duo or just want to eat like a king, this mouthwatering recipe is guaranteed to hit the spot.

1. Sprinkle the ground peppercorns evenly on both sides of the steaks. Use your hands or the flat side of a knife to press them onto the meat. Cover and let stand for 30 minutes.
2. Choose a pan to sear the meat—you'll want a large pan that will fit all the steaks without crowding them.
3. In your pan of choice, melt the butter and olive oil over medium-high heat until bubbling, about 1 minute.
4. Add the steaks and sear on each side until golden brown, about 6 minutes per side, or until they reach 135°F (57°C) on average.

5. Transfer cooked steaks to a plate and cover with foil.

6. Add the shallots to the pan, adding more butter, if necessary. Sauté for 2 to 3 minutes, or until softened.

7. Remove the pan from the heat and place the cognac in a ladle; use it to flame the shallots.

8. Add the wine, boil for about 3 minutes, until it thickens slightly.

9. Add the stock, bring to a boil again, and cook for 5 more minutes, or until the liquid is reduced by half and thickened, taking the consistency of a sauce.

10. Add the cream and mustard; stir, and simmer for 1 more minute.

11. Season with salt and pepper to taste.

12. To serve, cut the steaks in strips and transfer them to heated individual dishes. Bathe them with the sauce; garnish with parsley, and serve.

POLLO ASADO

MAKES
10
servings

5 pounds (2.3 kg) boneless, skinless chicken breasts

10 teaspoons (44 g) Lawry's Casero Pollo Asado seasoning

1 tablespoon (15 ml) olive oil (optional)

While traveling from Mexico to Michigan and all points in between to document lucha events, photographer Jerry Villagrana doesn't always have the time to cook a proper meal. Happily, he still gets to eat well because he's a maestro of meal prep and pollo asado is his go-to dish.

This easy-to-prepare recipe is high in protein but low in fat and carbs, perfect for keeping Villagrana energized on long shoots. It's also a flexible protein option that can be used in salads, tacos, or any number of dishes. He makes this recipe on a weekly basis; once you try it, you might, too.

NOTE: This recipe can be made ahead. The chicken will keep for 3 to 4 days in the fridge, or up to 3 months in the freezer. Villagrana recommends cutting the chicken into strips before storing so it's easily accessible as a snack or as a protein in meals.

1. Working with one chicken breast at a time, place each chicken breast in a resealable plastic bag and pound until the breast has an even thickness, which will ensure even cooking.
2. Season each breast with 2 teaspoons of seasoning.
3. Heat an outdoor grill to high. Once hot, place the chicken on the grill. Grill for about 8 minutes on each side, or until it has reached an internal temperature of 165°F (73°C).

4. Alternatively, you can cook the chicken indoors in a saucepan; cooking may take longer. Heat the pan on medium high and lightly oil with the olive oil. Place the chicken in the pan and cook for 5 to 6 minutes per side.

5. Remove the chicken from the grill or saucepan; let rest for 5 minutes before cutting the meat or serving to preserve moisture.

See pages 80–85 for Jerry Villagrana's story and Carne Asada Street Tacos.

JOSE "EL POLLO" GIL

 GUADALAJARA, MEXICO

MASKS ARE THE basic cornerstone of lucha libre, with luchadores creating masks that represent them and, in turn, inspiring fans with their masks. Many fans have become so enthralled with lucha libre that they have amassed huge collections of masks from their favorite luchadores. El Pollo, one of the lucha libre industry's top photographers, has a legendary collection of masks that cover nearly every inch of the walls of his "lucha cave."

Originally from Guadalajara, Mexico, El Pollo's life as a collector started at a young age when a friend of luchador Septiembre Negro gave him a mask the star had worn in a match. Attending the weekly matches every Sunday at Arena Coliseo in Guadalajara, he would pick up the simple fan or commercial-grade masks with money from his allowance. When he moved to the United States, he attended a FMLL event at which one of his childhood idols, Atlantis, was wrestling. He saw that Atlantis was selling masks and purchased one

directly from him, then he followed that by purchasing masks from Fishman, El Hijo del Santo, Blue Demon Jr., and Mascara Sagrada Jr.

El Pollo's collection spans well over one hundred masks with a large percentage of those masks coming directly from the luchador. When asked what some of his favorites were, he mentioned a mask given to him as a gift from Mascara Sagrada and the last mask that Fishman wore while wrestling in Japan, along with masks worn by Blue Demon Jr., Lizmark, the mask worn by Pentagón Jr. when he faced Prince Puma at a *Lucha Underground* taping, and the mask of El Torito that he wore while he was wrestling for WWE, which the superstar gave him as a gift.

El Pollo's philosophy is to collect masks that you really want and to always try to get them from the luchadores directly. Although that may not be very easy for the average fan, with El Pollo continuing to shoot photos ringside for leading lucha libre website LuchaCentral.com and Mexico-based magazine *Box y Lucha*, he will continue to find himself in the right place at the right time. (For anyone who wants more advice on how to start their own epic mask collections, Dos Hermanos Lucha [page 188] have a podcast called *The Mask Cast with Dos Hermanos Lucha* dedicated to this very topic.)

POLLO-LESS MOLCAJETE

SERVES
2

5 tomatillos

2 serrano peppers

½ habanero chile

Pinch of salt

1 chicken bouillon cube

1 tablespoon (15 ml) vegetable oil

2 nopale (cactus) pads, spines
removed

4 small shallots

2 medium-cut flap steaks

12 ounces (340 g) pork chorizo

8 ounces (225 g) jumbo shrimp,
peeled and deveined

8 ounces (225 g) queso Oaxaca,
pulled into strings

2 slices panela cheese

8 small corn tortillas, for serving

1 avocado, peeled, pitted, and
sliced, for serving

Jose Gil isn't just famous for being one of the top lucha libre photographers in the US—he's also famous for his deep detestation of chicken! In fact, he despises this popular poultry so much that he's even earned himself a tongue-in-cheek nickname: El Pollo.

His wife, Carla Gil (aka Mrs. Pollo), was inspired to make this dish after she saw a molcajete in a restaurant window. The only problem? Many traditional molcajete dishes contain chicken, so she'd have to come up with her own recipe. She concocted this chicken-free dish, and it quickly became a favorite dinner when Jose came home after a long day of photographing.

1. Make the salsa: In a saucepan, bring 2 cups (475 ml) of water to a boil. Add the tomatillos, peppers, and a pinch of salt; boil for 10 minutes.

2. Remove from the heat; let cool briefly, then transfer to a blender. Blend until smooth. Return the mixture to the saucepan, heating over low heat. Add the bouillon cube and stir occasionally. Keep the mixture hot.

3. On a large, flat skillet, heat the oil toward one side. Add the nopales and shallots. Place the steak and chorizo on the other side of the skillet. Cook for 8 to 10 minutes over medium heat.

4. Add the shrimp to the chorizo. Cook for about 5 more minutes, or until all is at your desired level of doneness.

5. Put a molcajete (pestle and mortar) upside down on the stovetop over high heat for about 5 minutes. While waiting for the molcajete to heat up, remove the meat, shrimp, cactus, and chorizo from the pan. Cut a fringe into each piece, not cutting through (each piece should look like an open hand).

6. Carefully remove the hot molcajete from the stove and place on a flat dish. Add the Oaxaca strings. Carefully pour the salsa on top of the cheese—it should sizzle! Add the meat, chorizo, shrimp, cactus, shallots, and panela slices.

7. Serve with warm tortillas and sliced avocado.

BLACK TAURUS

 FROM **TORREÓN, COAHUILA, MEXICO** ♦ **DEBUT** **NOVEMBER 2005**

A FIFTEEN-YEAR PRO, BLACK Taurus is what we'd call the textbook definition of the phrase "when you mess with the bull, you get the horns." With a terrifying horned mask and a look straight out of Conan the Barbarian, it's hard not to be intimidated by Black Taurus when he looks at you. That the Lucha Libre AAA luchador can outbrawl, overpower, outwrestle, and even outfly his opponents (regardless of size) just makes it all the more dire when an opponent gets in the ring with him. Just ask former UFC Heavyweight Champion Cain Velasquez. The Mexican MMA fighter made his lucha libre debut in a match that saw him lock horns with the wily vet.

FUN FACTS

* Black Taurus received training from noted maestro and lucha libre legend El Satánico.
* He's wrestled for every major lucha libre organization in Mexico, including Lucha Libre AAA and Consejo Mundial de Lucha Libre (CMLL), the oldest wrestling promotion in the world. The year 2019 was a breakout year for Black Taurus in the US and 2020 saw him wrestle in Germany's top tournament of the year, the WXW 16 Carat.

* He began his career in CMLL under the name Semental. When he jumped to Lucha Libre AAA in 2012, he was a scary-looking rock star luchador named Machine Rocker before becoming a menacing bull. Originally he was simply called Taurus, but when he left AAA to make it on his own as an independent, he added Black to his name. Now back in AAA as a top heavyweight, people often refer to him as either.

PORK LOIN WITH MANGO SALSA

SERVES 2

1 pound (455 g) pork loin, washed and dried

1 tablespoon (18 g) kosher salt

1 tablespoon (6 g) ground white pepper

6 tablespoons (84 g) unsalted butter

2 tablespoons (19 g) minced garlic

1 teaspoon (1 g) minced onion

2 cups (400 g) mango puree

1 medium-size red bell pepper, seeded and julienned

1 medium-size yellow bell pepper, seeded and julienned

3 asparagus stalks

½ baguette

Care for some sweet with your meat? To some, the idea of combining savory and sweet might seem unusual. If that sounds like you, let this recipe for pork loin with mango salsa make you a believer.

Pork loin cooked with salt and pepper and plenty of butter and aromatics would make a satisfying meal on its own, but here it's transformed into a tropical getaway of a dinner once combined with homemade mango salsa and sautéed veggies. With a hunk of baguette on the side, this dish makes for a memorable meal.

1. Season the pork loin with the salt and white pepper.
2. In a saucepan over medium heat, melt 4 tablespoons (56 g) of the butter. Add half the garlic and onion; cook for about 2 minutes until browned, then add the pork loin. Cook for about 15 minutes, turning occasionally.
3. In a separate saucepan over medium heat, melt 1 tablespoon (14 g) of the butter. Add the remaining garlic and onion; cook for about 2 minutes, or until browned, then add the mango puree and heat briefly. Let the mixture cool, then transfer to a blender.
4. In a separate saucepan over medium heat, melt the remaining tablespoon (14 g) of butter. Add the bell peppers and asparagus and sauté until softened.
5. To serve, place pork loin on a plate, add mango salsa on top, asparagus and peppers on the side, and portions of baguette.

KIKUTARO

FROM · **OSAKA, JAPAN** · DEBUT · **JULY 1994**

KIKUTARO HAS HAD a long career in wrestling and has worn many hats, both figuratively and literally. Starting his career in Japan, he gained experience working for companies known for their hard-core, often bloody death matches, such as FMW, BJW, and IWA Japan. From there, he moved to Japanese independent companies, such as Osaka Pro Wrestling and DDT Pro-Wrestling. Osaka Pro was heavily influenced by lucha libre, whereas DDT had more of a comedic flair to it.

While working for Osaka Pro Wrestling, he took on the character Ebessan, which was based on the Japanese god of laughter, Ebisu. The costume he wore resembled lucha libre star Súper Muñeco, who was aimed at entertaining children. He wore a mask that had very large ears and clownlike features. During his matches he would mimic famous wrestlers by copying their biggest moves and mannerisms as part of his routine.

When he left Osaka Pro Wrestling, he was required to give up the Ebessan persona, which led him to create his own character, which is how Kikutaro was born. Kikutaro's appearance was very much like Ebessan, this time with a sideways hat attached to his mask and wearing a baseball jersey. His parodies of wrestlers ran the gambit of favorites from his childhood such as Abdullah the Butcher, Jushin Liger, and Riki Choshu, to more modern-day stars, such as the Great Muta, Bret "The Hitman" Hart, and Mick Foley. His parodies would not only involve using the moves of his favorite wrestlers; he would also change his name as a tribute to those wrestlers.

Kikutaro is also very good friends with Japanese wrestler Nosawa, who not only competed in Lucha Libre AAA for a period but also runs at least one major event in Tokyo each year to which he brings a few lucha legends and up-and-coming stars to Japan. Kikutaro often works those events and he also serves as a talent scout (sometimes officially, sometimes unofficially) for many of the Japanese companies for which he performs.

In the early 2000s, he brought his talents to the US, where he stepped into the ring with wrestling's rising stars. Kikutaro continues to bring

laughter and joy to wrestling rings around the globe. Today, he splits his time between Japan and the US, where he resides in Las Vegas and makes appearances for independent companies all over the country.

FUN FACTS

* Kikutaro competed for Consejo Mundial de Lucha Libre in 1997 when the promotion did a tour of Japan.

* He's also wrestled under the names Ebessan, Ebessan Hansen, Kikusan Hansen, Ebetaro, Kikuzawa, KIKUZAWA (yes, the same as the last name, only in all caps), Mitsunobu Kikujawa, Ebedullah the Butcher, Ebisu Yellow, Blue Fire Kikuzo, and his real name, Mitsonobu Kikuzawa.

* He's held twelve championships, including eleven reigns as the Dramatic Dream Team's (DDT) Ironman Heavymetalweight Champion.

PORK BELLY AND GINGER HOT POT

SERVES
2 to 3

1 head napa (Chinese) cabbage

8 ounces (225 g) pork belly, cut into ¼ x 1½-inch (6 mm x 4 cm)-wide portions

3 (1-ounce [28 g]) pieces fresh ginger, shredded

1½ cups (288 g) chicken bouillon powder, plus more to taste

OPTIONAL ADD-INS:

Shiitake mushrooms, sliced

King oyster mushrooms, sliced

Garlic, thinly sliced

Soft tofu, cut into 1-inch (2.5 cm) cubes

Kikutaro isn't just a luchador—he's a full-fledged personality and a foodie to boot. He even has his own cooking channel on YouTube. Give it a Google; it's guaranteed to make your day.

This is one of Kikutaro's go-to recipes, as it's simple to make, adaptable in any number of ways, and is highly comforting and restorative. As Kikutaro sums it up, "Very good for if you have a cold or flu, or just need to recover from being worn down from life on the road."

1. By hand, rip the cabbage into large pieces, about 3 inches (7.5 cm) long.
2. Place the torn portions in the bottom of a large cooking pot, completely lining the bottom of the pot with two layers. You'll have cabbage left over; set aside.
3. Add the pork on top of the cabbage. Add about one-third of the ginger on top of the pork. Sprinkle about ½ cup (96 g) of the chicken bouillon powder on top.
4. If using, add about a third of the mushrooms. If using, add about a third of the garlic.
5. Cover with another layer of cabbage; push down firmly with your hand so you can fit more ingredients in the pot.

✳ 218 ✳

6. Repeat the layering process with all the ingredients. You may have two or three layers. If adding tofu, add it last. Finish with a final layer of cabbage. Add the remaining cup (192 g) of chicken bouillon powder to the pot. Add 1 cup (240 ml) of water, cover, and heat over medium heat. Simmer for about 15 minutes, until the ginger is fully cooked and no longer has a strong odor.

7. Increase heat and bring liquid to a boil and let the mixture cook for about 45 minutes. Give it a taste; if you want more flavor, add more chicken bouillon powder. If it's too strong, add up to ½ cup (120 ml) more water.

8. Serve in a bowl; to be traditional, eat with chopsticks.

FULGOR I & FULGOR II

 MEXICO CITY, MEXICO

FULGOR I: **JUNE 2008**

FULGOR II: **JUNE 2009**

WHILE IT MAY look weird to someone not familiar with lucha libre to have two people with the same name and simply number them as if they came off the pages of a Dr. Seuss book, it is, in fact, not an uncommon way to distinguish a tag team, especially one with real-life brothers. Not a whole lot is known about Fulgor I and Fulgor II—also not too uncommon for masked men! What is known is that they are indeed brothers who broke into the lucha business under the tutelage of one of the sport's most legendary trainers, Black Terry. As such, the siblings have been a fixture on the lucha libre indies, primarily plying their craft as the tag team Los Fulgores in the International Wrestling Revolution Group. You can largely find Fulgor I and Fulgor II working as dastardly rudos against some of IWRG's up-and-coming high flyers.

FUN FACTS

* Although tag team gold has continued to elude them, Fulgor I has won two singles championships.
* Family members include fellow independent luchadores Serpiente Azteca and Camaleon Sting.
* The Fulgor name translates to "glare."

POZOLE

SERVES
10 to 14

9 pounds (4 kg) pork skirt and rib (on the bone), cut into chunks

3 medium-size white onions, coarsely chopped

3 garlic cloves, finely chopped

1 tablespoon (18 g) kosher salt

3.5 ounces (100 g) guajillo chile

9 pounds (4 kg) hominy, cooked and cooled

TO SERVE (OPTIONAL AND TO TASTE):

Chopped or sliced radishes

Dried oregano

Grated cheese (queso fresco or Cotija)

Chili powder

Chopped lettuce or cabbage

Chopped onion

Sour cream

Limes

Tostadas

Pozole is synonymous with celebration and good times with family or friends. It's most traditionally served around the holidays, so you're unlikely to find recipes with a small yield—it's designed to feed a crowd. For Fulgor I and Fulgor II, it's a holiday tradition; they usually cook it to celebrate Mexican Independence Day.

With this recipe, slow-cooked hominy is rendered absolutely flavor-filled with a mixture of fatty pork, garlic, onions, and chile. You can personalize the experience by serving it with a variety of garnishes—each eater can choose their own adventure in terms of garnishing and creating their own personalized experience.

1. In a large pot, combine 4 gallons (15 L) of water with the pork, onions, garlic, and salt.

2. Bring to a low boil and let cook for about 1 hour.

3. Skim the top and remove the foam. Add more water to fill the pot again.

4. In a blender, combine the guajillo chile with 2 cups of the broth from the pot and blend to liquefy.

5. Add the mixture back to the pot and stir to combine. Cook for an additional 30 minutes.

6. Add the cooked hominy. Cook for an additional 30 minutes, then check pork for tenderness. It should come apart easily in your hands.

7. Serve in bowls and add garnishes or accompaniments to taste.

What is pozole?

In Mexico, pozole is a hearty soup traditionally eaten with tostadas topped with sour cream and grated cheese on the side.

PSYCHOSIS

 TIJUANA, BAJA CALIFORNIA, MEXICO • **MARCH 1989**

ONE OF THE luchadores who introduced American pro wrestling fans in the mid-'90s to the high-flying lucha libre style, Psychosis has spent the last three decades wrestling everywhere around the world from the bullrings of Mexico to WWE's WrestleMania and back. His given name is Dionicio Castellanos Torres and he was born May 19, 1971, in Tijuana, Mexico. Nicho, as he was then known, began training to be a luchador at the young age of sixteen at the famous Gimnasio de Tijuana. His trainers were his brother, luchador Fobia, and Tijuana legend Rey Misterio Sr.

His brother, Felipe Castellanos Torres, had been wrestling for a few years around the Baja California region. As the younger brother, Nicho would tag along as his older brother worked on his craft and eventually started training himself. That tiny TJ gym at the time would be home to a group of luchadores who would go on to change not only the perception of lucha libre outside Mexico but also influence the style of pro wrestling around the world. Under the tutelage of Misterio Sr. you had a young Psychosis and very young Rey Misterio Jr.

(now Rey Mysterio), as well as Konnan El Bárbaro, Damian 666, and other future stars.

After a few years gaining experience, Nicho quickly rose to fame awing fans around the world, often standing across the ring from Rey Jr. Their matches were like something few had seen before. The two were going out and having state-of-the-art matches each and every night. The success of their matches spread like wildfire to become one of the most in demand matches at the time. For fans in the US, their first impression of Psychosis came when WCW co-promoted AAA's *When Worlds Collide* on November 6, 1994, on pay-per-view.

The next year, they would head to Japan and wow audiences; the course of pro wrestling history would forever be changed when Extreme Championship Wrestling was searching for fresh talent and Konnan, who had recently been on an overseas tour with some of the ECW producers, recommended Rey Misterio Jr. and Psychosis. For a few months in late 1995, the two opened eyes and dropped jaws, and from that moment forward, lucha libre would become part of the fabric of American pro wrestling.

In 1996, Psychosis and Rey were hired by Ted Turner's World Championship Wrestling, allowing their fame to expand far beyond North America and into one hundred–plus countries throughout the globe. While working for WCW, Psychosis captured the WCW World Cruiserweight Championship on April 19, 1999, defeating Rey Misterio Jr., Juventud Guerrera, and Blitzkrieg in a four-way match.

Psychosis was famous for his mask, which had horns coming out the sides of it and his long hair coming out the top. When a luchador loses his mask, it can be a career- and life-defining moment. Oftentimes, a luchador never rises to the same level of popularity afterward. Because, at the time, the Mexico and US wrestling worlds were still a bit further apart than they are in the age of YouTube and social media, Psychosis had two of these defining moments. His first apuestas match took place August 26, 1999, at his home arena, Auditorio de Tijuana, against his trainer, Rey Misterio Sr., who had his nephew Rey Misterio Jr. in his corner. Psychosis would lose to his trainer, who would continue to hold the record for most apuestas wins, as this was his twenty-sixth. To this day, no other Tijuana luchador has more apuestas wins. One month later, on the September 27, 1999, episode of WCW *Monday Nitro*, Psychosis lost his mask against Billy Kidman—this time revealing his face and identity, not in front of only thousands in the arena in TJ, but in front of millions of fans watching TV around the world.

He left WCW in 2000 and would travel the world wrestling for top US independent promotions, such as ECW and XPW, and overseas for All Japan and World Wrestling All-Stars. Sometimes, lucha libre names, masks, and rights become a cloudy issue. With Nicho now unmasked, but still called Psychosis (this being the WCW spelling of his name), back in Mexico, Lucha Libre AAA, the company in which he gained much of his early fame, decided to debut another wrestler under the name Psicosis (the original Mexico/real Spanish spelling of his name). To avoid confusion, the original Psychosis switched his name to Nicho el Millonario while continuing to crisscross the globe wrestling.

On June 12, 2005, WWE brought Psychosis in under that name to appear at their ECW One Night Stand pay-per-view to once again wrestle his longtime rival Rey Misterio Jr. Their match was so impressive that WWE offered him a full-time contract. This would lead to the formation of a stable known as the Mexicools on the WWE Smackdown brand, which would consist of Psychosis, his fellow early AAA/ECW groundbreaking luchador Juventud Guerrera (page 110), and ECW mainstay Super Crazy.

As the decade continued, he would return to Mexico first to CMLL and then back to his first major promotion, AAA. Some of his famous lucha de apuestas matches from this time would include teaming with his La Familia de Tijuana friends, Halloween and Damian 666 (page 196). They lost their hair putting it up against the masks of Los Psychos Circuses's masks on October 9, 2011, in Monterrey. The next year at Triplemanía XX, he put his hair against the hair of Joe Lider in front of more than twenty thousand fans at Arena Ciudad de Mexico and took the hair of Lider.

Throughout the 2010s, Nicho would continue to wrestle all around the globe and have notable runs on and off in AAA and then for Tijuana-based group The Crash. All the years of high-flying moves and top-rope leg drops did a number on both of his knees, and in 2018, he underwent major knee surgery on both legs.

He would return to action in 2019 and it was like years were taken off his body in a positive way. Nicho was moving around the ring as he had not been able to for most of the last decade. In 2020, wrestling fans round the globe joined Masked Republic in celebrating the twenty-fifth anniversary of the arrival of Psychosis, Rey Misterio Jr., Juventud Guerrera, and Konnan in ECW and the lasting impact on the entire pro wrestling business those few months in 1995 would have. A career that has spanned more than three decades, a mask revered as one of the most important in modern lucha libre history, Psychosis will go down in history as a true legend of lucha libre.

SPANISH TORTILLA

MAKES
2 to 4
servings

5 ounces (150 ml) extra-virgin
   olive oil

2¼ pounds (1 kg) potatoes, peeled
   and thinly sliced

6 large eggs, lightly beaten

2 teaspoons (12 g) kosher salt

Don't be fooled by the name: There are no actual tortillas in this recipe. A Spanish tortilla is actually more like an omelet, and it works equally well for brunch, a casual dinner, or, if you're a luchador, as a satisfying snack after a match. That is to say, it's always the right time for this recipe.

This dish is a favorite of legendary luchador Psychosis. He picked it up from popular Tijuana chef and nutritionist Ittoh Rodríguez, who has befriended—and cooked for—many of the top luchadores in the region. He loves that it's easy enough to make with his son Kevin, and the results are delicious and satisfying. No wonder it's become their go-to recipe.

1. In a large saucepan, heat the oil for 2 to 3 minutes, or until shimmering. Add the potatoes and fry over low heat for about 5 minutes, until softened and lightly browned.

2. Increase the heat to high; add the eggs and salt. Cook for about 10 minutes, or until browned and crispy; flip and cook the second side. Serve hot.

TINIEBLAS JR.

 MEXICO CITY, MEXICO ◆ **JUNE 1990**

TINIEBLAS JR. IS a second-generation luchador who had massive shoes to fill. His father, Tinieblas Sr., is one of the most famous luchadores from the 1970s through the 1990s and into today—impressive considering he started his career in his thirties. What made the elder Tinieblas stand out despite his late start was his unique look—at 6 foot 3 (190.5 cm), 240 pounds (109 kg), the former bodybuilder was one of the most impressive physical specimens ever seen in lucha libre during his day. This helped his second career as an actor, as he appeared in numerous lucha libre films and even had a run as a comic book hero—the first luchador in history to do so after the legendary El Santo, who introduced the trend. With all that his father has accomplished, it was a lot for Tinieblas Jr. to measure up to.

Fortunately, Tinieblas Jr. has been up to the challenge ever since he made his debut in 1990. As equally an imposing figure as his father at 6 foot 4 (193 cm) and 238 pounds (108 kg), Tinieblas Jr.

has had successful runs in the Universal Wrestling Association, Consejo Mundial de Lucha Libre, and especially Lucha Libre AAA during the '90s, where he proved himself to be a better overall talent than the elder Tinieblas (in fairness, he started at a younger age than his father did). Even in his fifties, Tinieblas has continued to go strong, adapting the same strategy as his father by employing his father's sidekick Alushe—a fuzzy Mayan elf—as his comedic partner in crime. With Alushe accompanying Tinieblas Jr. almost everywhere he wrestles, the act has practically become inseparable. Tinieblas Jr. is also a successful promoter of lucha libre events with his company FULL, which produces live shows throughout Mexico, bringing lucha libre to the masses.

On top of lucha libre, Tinieblas Jr. has also followed his father's path out of the ring by transitioning into other forms of entertainment. The heir to the Tinieblas legacy not only stars in The Luchaverse with the Tinieblas Jr. comic book series but also in his first feature film, *A 3 Caidas*.

SURF AND TURF (DARKNESS OF LAND AND SEA)

SERVES
3
(or 1 very hungry luchador)

- 1 cup (195 g) uncooked white rice
- 1 cup (84 g) rotini pasta
- 3 large eggs
- 1 cup (150 g) cherry tomatoes
- 1 carrot, grated
- 3 tablespoons (45 ml) vegetable oil
- 8 ounces (225 g) butterflied chicken breast
- 9 ounces (225 g) tilapia fillet
- 1 bell pepper, seeded and sliced

Surf and turf might seem like a fancy, restaurant-only sort of affair, but this recipe from the famous Tinieblas Jr. proves that it can be easy to prepare.

Protein, starch, and salad form a food pyramid–friendly dinner that's easy to make and will satisfy even a luchador's hungriest appetite. Satisfy your food pyramid demands and fuel yourself for your next lucha match (whether to participate or just watch) with this recipe from a legendary luchador.

1. In one pot, cook the rice in 1 cup (240 ml) of water over low heat for 20 minutes.
2. In a second pot, cook the pasta in 2 cups (475 ml) of water over high heat for 10 minutes.
3. In a third pot, boil the eggs in 1 cup (240 ml) of water over high heat for 5 minutes.
4. Once cooked, drain the water from each pot.
5. Transfer the rice to a bowl; set aside. Peel and dice the eggs.
6. Transfer the pasta to a large bowl; stir in and combine the eggs, cherry tomatoes, and grated carrot.

7. In a large saucepan, heat the vegetable oil over medium-high heat.

8. Fry the chicken steak, fish fillet, and peppers for about 8 minutes, or until they have achieved your desired level of doneness.

9. Assemble your plate into portions: chicken, fish, and peppers; pasta salad; and rice as desired.

HADES

 MADERO, TAMAULIPAS, MEXICO ◆ **NOVEMBER 2011**

WITH NEARLY A decade of experience under her belt, Hades got her break in the lucha libre world when she appeared on Lucha Libre AAA's Llave a la Gloria reality challenge in 2017. Her performances were enough to get her in a dark (nontelevised) match at the company's biggest show of the year, Triplemanía XXV, and even an appearance at another major event, Héroes Inmortales, a few months later. She returned to the independents throughout 2018 but then reemerged in AAA in late 2019 during their Lucha Capital competition. This would truly be her *big* break as she would have a series of show-stealing performances against the likes of Ayako Hamada, Big Mami, La Hiedra, and Lady Shani, many of the biggest names in AAA's luchadoras division. You have to be pretty good to hang with performers like that, and fortunately the twenty-six-year-old luchadora is as talented as they come, especially when she decides to fly. Ever since the tournament, she's been a regular on AAA undercards.

FUN FACTS

* Hades was part of a Llave a la Gloria (Lucha Libre AAA reality-style competition to find a new superstar) class that included Ángel Mortal Jr. (La Parka Negra), Angelikal (Myzteziz Jr.), Pardux (La Parkita Negra), Villano III Jr., and El Hijo del Vikingo.

* She came up under the name Hahastary, which she continues to use on the independent circuit.
* She was the second holder of the IWP's Women's Championship, winning it in 2015.

TINGA DE ZANAHORIA

SERVES
2 to 4

1 medium-size white onion, chopped into ¼-inch (6 mm) pieces

Vegetable oil, for frying

8 medium-size carrots, peeled and grated into strips

½ large tomato, sliced

1 (1-ounce [25 g]) can chipotle chilies

1 garlic clove, finely chopped

Kosher salt

TO SERVE (OPTIONAL AND TO TASTE):

Sour cream

5 tostadas

Grated cheese (Mexican Manchego or queso Chihuahua preferred, but Monterrey Jack is okay.)

Grated lettuce

You won't *carrot* all that there's no meat in this main dish! While *tinga*—a dish composed of tostadas served with tasty toppings—is traditionally prepared with chicken or meat, this version is made with carrot to suit luchadora Hahastary's (aka Hades in Lucha Libre AAA) vegetarian diet.

Prepared with a mélange of flavorful veggies and aromatics, and served with plenty of creamy sauce and cheese, you won't miss the meat with this hearty veg-friendly dish. To make this recipe vegan, omit the sour cream and cheese or use vegan varieties.

1. In a large saucepan, fry half the onion in oil over medium heat for about 3 minutes, until golden brown.

2. Add the grated carrots and cook, stirring occasionally, for about 8 minutes, or until lightly browned and softened. Remove from the heat and set aside.

3. In a blender, combine the tomatoes, chipotle chiles, garlic, and remaining onion. Add salt to taste and add enough water to cover the ingredients. Blend until smooth.

4. Pour the sauce on top of the carrot mixture in the pan and bring to a boil over medium-high heat. Lower the heat to a simmer and cook for 8 to 10 minutes, or until thickened.

5. To serve, drizzle sour cream on top of a tostada, sprinkle with cheese and lettuce, and top with the carrot mixture.

DRIZZLE WITH SOUR CREAM TO SERVE.

YOU
WON'T
MISS
the meat
in this dish!

AMY DUMAS

 FORT LAUDERDALE, FL ♦ **JANUARY 1999**

AMY DUMAS HAS a unique entry into professional wrestling, with direct ties to the world of lucha libre and Mexico. Her Hall of Fame career started by watching such luchadores as Rey Misterio Jr. on WCW's *Monday Nitro*. Their colorful costumes and high-flying matches inspired her to leave home in Washington, DC, and head for Mexico City without having any prior knowledge of lucha libre. Her mission: seek out training to become a luchador.

When she first arrived, she attended events at Arena Coliseo and Arena México, in the process gaining the attention of the promoters of CMLL. They gave her an opportunity to appear as a valet (someone who accompanies a wrestler to the ring and at times may get involved in the action) for different luchadores, but that wasn't enough for Amy; she wanted to get into the ring and compete.

Here she was, a young American in Mexico, without a job and very little money, living in a foreign country doing whatever she could to learn as much as she could about lucha libre. While there, Amy became friendly with some of the American wrestlers who were working for CMLL. They took her under their wing and gave her some fundamental training in the art of lucha libre. She would go on to visit Mexico numerous times to learn as much as she could.

When she returned to the US, Amy continued learning how to wrestle, which led her to make some appearances with ECW, before being noticed and getting hired by WWE and given the name Lita.

Art would then imitate life when, more than two years after returning from Mexico and changing her focus to training in traditional American pro wrestling, Amy would be paired with luchador Essa Ríos for her WWE debut. Her alliance with Rios was short lived, but the connection with the fans was not. Next, she teamed up with her Team Extreme partners Matt and Jeff Hardy, and this is when she really broke out as a major WWE Superstar. Lita would go on to hold the WWE Women's Championship a remarkable four times.

When Amy stepped away from competing in the ring full time in 2006, she entered the world of punk rock. Along with her bandmates, she created

a group called the Luchagors whose name was inspired by her love of lucha libre and monster movies. The Luchagors recorded a self-titled album under the Hellcat Records label and toured briefly.

Lita has made numerous returns to WWE, including at the 2018 Royal Rumble, and makes public appearances at conventions like the 2019 Expo Lucha event in San Diego, where she reunited with Essa Ríos for the first time in nearly twenty years. In 2014, Lita was inducted into the WWE Hall of Fame.

TLACOYO DE NOPAL

YIELDS
2
Nopales

TINGA SAUCE:

3 medium-size red tomatoes, coarsely chopped

¼ medium-size white onion, coarsely chopped

1 tablespoon (7 g) chipotle chile powder

NOPALES:

4 teaspoons (20 ml) vegetable oil

1 medium-size white onion, thinly sliced

1 medium-size carrot, peeled and ends removed, grated

Salt

4 nopales, washed and dried

½ cup (116 g) previously cooked refried beans

2 medium-size red tomatoes, diced

2 large avocados, peeled, pitted, and sliced

Freshly ground black pepper

Fresh cilantro

Long before she ever stepped foot into an American ring, Amy Dumas lived and trained in Mexico. Her evening ritual? Testing her Spanish by ordering from the various street food vendors in the area, trying to find something to suit her vegetarian diet. It was through these adventures that she first sampled nopales in Mexico City. These days, she lives in San Francisco, where she still buys nopales at her corner bodega to prepare this memory-evoking dish.

1. Make the tinga sauce: In a pot filled with 6½ cups (1.5 L) of water, boil the tomatoes and onion over medium-high heat for 10 minutes. Transfer to a blender, add the chipotle chile powder, and blend to liquefy.

2. Use a strainer to remove all large pieces; set the sauce aside.

3. Make the nopales: In a large saucepan, heat 3 tablespoons of oil over high heat. Add the sliced onion; cook for about 3 minutes, until soft.

4. Add the carrot and the tinga sauce. Add salt to taste. Cook for 10 to 15 minutes.

5. Remove the mixture from the pan and set aside.

6. Using the same pan, heat 1 teaspoon (5 ml) of vegetable oil over medium heat; add the nopales and cook until soft, about 10 minutes per side.

7. Transfer the cooked nopales to serving plates; layer with refried beans and the carrot tinga. Add diced tomatoes, avocado slices, salt, pepper, and cilantro to taste.

ZOKRE

 LOS ANGELES, CA ◆ **AUGUST 2000**

ZOKRE, WHO IS one half of the tag-team Los Luchas (with Phoenix Star), is best known for his work in Pro Wrestling Guerrilla and throughout the Southern California independent pro wrestling scene. He began his career in 2002 after training at the world-famous Gil's Garage and Revolution Pro's Rudos Dojo.

In the lucha libre tradition of portraying one character before you come into your own and take on your more permanent identity, Zokre began his career in a chicken costume as part of the team of Los Gallineros (as have a number of other wrestlers who came up through RevPro and the Rudos Dojo). Known for their innovative style of wrestling, Matt Jackson of the Young Bucks has listed Los Luchas as a major influence on their career.

Today, Zokre can still be found wrestling in Southern California as well as training new wrestlers in lucha libre at the Santino Bros. Wrestling Academy. He's had a hand in training many of today's fastest rising stars, including Ring of Honor's Brody King, Major League Wrestling's Douglas James, and WWE NXT's Jake Atlas.

FUN FACTS

★ Other wrestlers to have started their careers as a masked Gallinero include All Elite Wrestling's Scorpio Sky and Matt Jackson.

★ Zokre wrestled on the debut show of the now highly influential independent wrestling promotion Pro Wrestling Guerrilla, teaming with Ryan Drago (Simon Grimm) and Topgun Talwar.

★ He once held the NWA World Tag Team Championship with Phoenix Star.

PHOENIX STAR

ZOKRE

VEGETARIAN "CHICKEN" CHILE VERDE

SERVES
4

1½ pounds (680 g) tomatillo verde

3 whole jalapeño peppers, stems removed

3 garlic cloves, crushed

1 vegetable bouillon cube, smashed

1 cup (40 g) fresh cilantro

1 cup (30 g) fresh spinach

1 teaspoon (3 g) kosher salt

½ cup (120 ml) vegetable oil

4 medium-size Yukon Gold potatoes, cut into 1-inch (2.5 cm) cubes

1 (10-ounce [280 g]) bag meatless chicken strips

We all have childhood nostalgia for certain recipes, but as time goes on, preferences change. When Zokre went vegetarian, he lamented the loss of his mom's chicken chile verde, but the sorrow was short-lived: happily, she was able to modify it to suit his new lifestyle.

This recipe allows for plenty of personalization—do you prefer a chunkier texture? Cut, chop, and blend a little more coarsely. Prefer different spices or a different brand of meatless chicken? Go for it.

1. In a medium-size pot, combine 4 cups (946 ml) of water, tomatillo verde, and jalapeños. Cover and bring to a boil.

2. Remove from the heat and transfer to a blender. Add the garlic, vegetable bouillon cube, cilantro, spinach, and salt. Add 1 cup (240 ml) of water and blend to your desired consistency: more for a smooth consistency, less for a chunky consistency. Set aside.

3. In a medium-size saucepan, combine the vegetable oil and potatoes. Sauté over medium heat for 12 minutes, or until cooked through and tender in texture. Drain any excess oil and remove the potatoes from the pan.

4. Add the meatless chicken strips to the pan and sauté until crispy brown.

5. Add the potatoes to the pan. Add the tomatillo mixture. Simmer over low heat for 5 minutes, or until heated through. Let cool slightly; serve warm.

featuring

DESSERTS

★ CAIDA TRES ★

SUPER TASTY BACON JR.

 PORKOPIA, FIGHTING OUT OF LONDON, ENGLAND **JANUARY 2017**

BACON JR. ALWAYS likes to introduce himself as "the irresistible, irrepressible, incomparable man they call Super Tasty Bacon Jr." Hailing from Porkopia, he claims to be the son of King Bacon and out to prove he can follow in his father's footsteps by taking on Earth's greatest luchadores and wrestlers. The Savior of Flavor knows how to mix it up in the ring and loves to entertain the crowds at Lucha Britannia, the London Lucha League, and Vertigo Pro Wrestling.

FUN FACTS

* Super Tasty Bacon Jr. was the first London Lucha League (LLL) World Champion and has also held the Vertigo Pro World Championship.

* He was trained at the London School of Lucha Libre by Greg Burridge and Garry Vanderhorne.
* He loves ice cream nearly as much as he loves bacon.

CANDIED BACON AND PRETZEL BROWNIES

MAKES
16
pieces

CANDIED BACON:

2 tablespoons (40 g) honey, for
   drizzling

2 tablespoons (30 g) packed light
   brown sugar

4 strips bacon

BROWNIES:

Unsalted butter, for pan

3 ounces (85 g) unsweetened
   chocolate, roughly chopped

8 tablespoons (1 stick, 113 g)
   unsalted butter

1 1/3 cups (265 g) granulated sugar

2 large eggs, lightly beaten

1 teaspoon (5 ml) pure vanilla
   extract

1/2 teaspoon (2.4 g) flaky sea salt,
   or 1/4 teaspoon (1.5 g) table salt

2/3 cup (83 g) all-purpose flour

15 to 20 salted pretzels

It should come as no surprise that bacon is one of Super Tasty Bacon Jr.'s favorite foods. But he doesn't just limit it to savory consumption. As he puts it, "Bacon is grossly underrepresented when it comes to dessert . . . and I love dessert!"

Happily, Mama Bacon found a solution to this dire dilemma years ago by adding bacon to brownies, and over the years, Super Tasty Bacon has augmented the recipe in some spectacular ways, including taking the time to candy the bacon and adding an awesome crunch with pretzels. These brownies are truly unlike anything else!

NOTE: Super Tasty Bacon Jr. urges you to make this recipe your own. As he puts it, "You can add chili powder or black pepper to the candied bacon for extra kick or crunch up the pretzels and add them to the mix! Sometimes I replace the pretzels with pecans, or I make candied coffee beans and add those too."

1. Make the candied bacon: Preheat the oven to 375°F (190°C). Place a rack on top of a baking sheet. The rack will allow for even cooking of the bacon; the baking sheet below will catch the drippings.

248

2. Drizzle the honey and sprinkle the light brown sugar on a large, flat dish. Mix together (it's okay if the sugar is not totally dissolved). Rub the bacon strips in the gooey mixture, lightly coating both sides. Place the bacon on the rack above the baking sheet. Bake for 20 to 25 minutes, or until it's reached your desired level of crispiness. When done, gently remove the rack from the pan and let the bacon cool.

3. Make the brownies: Lower the oven temperature to 350°F (180°C). Position a rack in the middle position. Line an 8-inch (20.5 cm) square baking pan with parchment paper. Butter the parchment paper.

4. In a double boiler or a heatproof bowl atop a pot of simmering water, melt the chocolate and butter until the chocolate is mostly melted, 5 minutes. Remove from the heat and stir to melt any residual solid pieces.

5. Whisk in the granulated sugar, eggs, vanilla, and salt, mixing until the batter is mostly streak free. Stir in the flour with a spatula. Do not overmix.

6. By now, the bacon should be cool; chop or crumble it and fold it into the batter. Pour the batter into the prepared baking pan and decide how many brownies you want to make. Add pretzels on the top accordingly, so you'll have one pretzel per brownie once cut.

7. Bake for 25 to 30 minutes, or until a toothpick or knife inserted into the center comes out mostly clean.

8. Remove from the oven and let cool or go whole hog and serve them warm with a big scoop of vanilla ice cream.

EAT LIKE A
LUCHADOR

MARIACHI LOCO

 SAN SEBASTIAN EL GRANDE, JALISCO, MEXICO **SEPTEMBER 2008**

LIKE HIS LUCHA Homies partner Lil' Cholo (see page 148), Mariachi Loco got started on the SoCal scene before joining *Lucha Underground* as a mariachi singer, where the story was that LU owner and promoter Dario Cueto just happened to see him performing at a restaurant one night. During the show's four seasons, Loco effectively portrayed himself, Disciples of Death member Siniestro de la Muerte, and Rabbit Tribe member Saltador, where he became known for his unique checkered-patterned outfit. Still hanging out with Cholo all these years later, Loco is a mainstay of the Empire Wrestling Federation and Lucha VaVOOM, whose flamboyant presentation fits perfectly for a performer like Loco.

FUN FACTS

* Mariachi Loco is the only member of The Lucha Homies to hold Lucha Underground gold, having won the Lucha Underground Trios Championships as a member of the Disciples of Death.
* Has won three other championships in addition to the LU Trios titles, including the Empire Wrestling Federation Championship twice.

* Not only is Lil' Cholo his partner in The Lucha Homies tag team, but Cholo was actually one of his trainers, too, at WPW, a Southern California lucha libre promotion and school from which many luchadores have come.

250

FRESAS CON CREMA

SERVES
4

- 2¼ pounds (1 kg) fresh strawberries, hulled and cut into quarters
- 2 cups (460 g) sour cream
- 1 (14-ounce [397 g]) can sweetened condensed milk
- 2 teaspoons (10 ml) pure vanilla extract
- 1 tablespoon (12 g) granulated sugar
- 5 teaspoons (scant 12 g) ground cinnamon
- 8 thin wafer cookies (such as Pirouline cookies), for garnish

Luchador Mariachi Loco is known for bringing the party to his sport. His vibrant personality has made him a crowd favorite in Lucha VaVOOM and half a beloved luchador tag team with his "lucha homie" Lil' Cholo (see Cholo's story and recipe on pages 148–151).

He's also known for his love of dessert! *Fresas con crema*— a simple dessert made with fresh strawberries and a sweet cream mixture—was one of his favorite treats while growing up. Some things never change: he's still loco about this dessert, and once you try it, you will be too.

1. Place the chopped strawberries in a large bowl. Refrigerate.

2. In a separate large bowl, combine the sour cream, sweetened condensed milk, vanilla, sugar, and most of the cinnamon, reserving about 2 teaspoons (5 g) to sprinkle on top of the finished servings. Mix well to combine.

3. Fold in the strawberries. Serve in individual glasses or small bowls. Garnish with cookies and a sprinkle of cinnamon.

KEYRA

 TEPITO, MEXICO CITY, MEXICO ◆ **JANUARY 2009**

IT'S AMAZING TO think that Keyra already has more than ten years of experience in lucha libre, especially since she's only twenty-five years old. But with a no-nonsense attitude and great wrestling skills, all it means is that the well-rounded luchadora will continue to be one of the best performers in Mexico for years to come. And not just against her fellow women, either—Keyra is more than willing to take on all comers. Those who have accepted her challenge have quickly learned that she can more than hold her own. Although it is not completely uncommon for a luchador to be described as a "strong style" wrestler (very hard-hitting punches and kicks that make matches look and feel more like a real fight), Keyra is one of the top luchadoras in all of the sport who has been associated with that style of fighting.

FUN FACTS

★ Keyra was trained by legendary maestros Gran Apache and Virus.

★ She started training for lucha libre at only thirteen years old, which is not uncommon in Mexico, or even in lucha libre training in the US.

★ She has held *nine* championships in her career, including The Crash Women's Championship and arguably the most valuable women's title in all of lucha libre, Lucha Libre AAA's Reina de Reinas (Queen of Queens) Championship.

FRESH FRUIT TART

SERVES
8

CRUST:

1 ²/₃ cups (200 g) all-purpose flour

½ cup (100 g) sugar

8 tablespoons (1 stick, 113 g)
unsalted butter, cold, cut into
½-inch (1.3 cm) cubes

1 large egg yolk

1 tablespoon (15 ml) pure vanilla
extract

½ teaspoon (3 g) kosher salt

CUSTARD FILLING:

2 cups (475 ml) whole milk

½ vanilla bean pod

¹/₈ teaspoon (0.75 g) kosher salt

⁵/₈ cup (125 g) sugar

2 large egg yolks

6 tablespoons (48 g) cornstarch

TOPPING:

Seasonal fruits (berries, pineapple, peaches, pears, etc.)

4 ounces (115 g) apricot jam

It wouldn't be an overstatement to call Keyra a luchadora wunderkind—at the age of twenty-five she already has more than ten years' experience, and she's held nine championships. But her mad skills aren't limited to the ring: she's also an accomplished baker.

This elegant fresh fruit tart may look as if it comes from a pricey Parisian patisserie, but it's actually surprisingly easy to make at home. Creamy custard is the perfect canvas for any number of toppings. Tailor the tart to your liking by choosing your favorite mix of seasonal fruits to pile on top. Then share a slice with your bestie, as Keyra certainly does with her BFF/occasional rival, luchadora Lady Maravilla (see her story and recipe on pages 262–265).

1. Preheat the oven to 350°F (180°C).

2. Make the crust: Combine the flour, sugar, butter, egg yolk, 2 tablespoons (30 ml) of cold water, vanilla extract, and salt in a food processor. Pulse for about 1 minute, then knead with your hands until the mixture comes together into a cohesive mass.

3. Roll the dough into a circle; transfer to a 9-inch (23 cm)-diameter tart pan. Press the dough down evenly into the bottom and sides of the pan. Prick the bottom of the dough several times with the tines of a fork. Cover the dough with foil or parchment paper, and place uncooked rice or beans on top (this will prevent the dough from losing its shape).

4. Bake for 10 minutes. Remove from the oven and set aside.

5. Prepare the custard: In a saucepan, combine the milk, vanilla bean, and salt. Bring to a boil over medium heat; cook for 10 minutes, then turn off the heat and let the mixture infuse for about 10 minutes. Discard the vanilla bean, but keep the milk mixture in the saucepan.

6. In a bowl, combine the sugar and egg yolks. Whisk for about 5 minutes, or until fluffy. Add the cornstarch; mix until incorporated.

7. Over low heat, slowly add the egg mixture to the milk, cooking for 1 minute. Increase the heat to medium; bring to a boil and whisk constantly for 3 minutes. Remove from the heat and transfer the mixture to a bowl. Cover with plastic wrap, letting the plastic touch the top of the custard to keep it from forming a skin. Chill in the refrigerator for at least 2 hours.

8. To assemble, pour the chilled custard into a piping bag and pipe into the prebaked crust until full and smooth.

9. Decorate the top of the tart with fresh fruit.

10. Mix the apricot jam with 1½ tablespoons (22 ml) of water; brush on top of the fresh fruit to make it shine and keep it from browning.

11. Let chill for at least 30 minutes before serving.

MR. IGUANA

 CULIÁCAN, SINALOA, MEXICO ◆   **JULY 2009**

IT DOESN'T GET weirder than Mr. Iguana, a ten-year pro who definitely lives the gimmick. Painted green on the face and sporting more charisma than your average cold-blooded reptile, Mr. Iguana has quickly established himself as one of the most entertaining luchadores around, from Monterrey indie RIOT! to the big houses of Lucha Libre AAA. Frankly, he could probably spend the next decade or so making people laugh and riding that wave, which makes it all the more impressive that he's one of the best high flyers in lucha libre today.

FUN FACTS

★ Mr. Iguana briefly wrestled for Consejo Mundial de Lucha Libre in 2015 on its Guadalajara circuit.

★ He's often accompanied to the ring by Yezka, a stuffed animal lizard who Iguana frequently uses to play mind games against opponents.

★ He was able to parlay his popularity on social media into a contract with the top lucha libre company in all Mexico—Lucha Libre AAA.

MR. IGUANA'S SUGAR COOKIES

MAKES
12
cookies

4 cups (500 g) all-purpose flour, plus more for dusting

1 teaspoon (4.6 g) baking powder

6 tablespoons plus 1 teaspoon (about 90 g) unsalted butter, at room temperature

1 cup (200 g) sugar

2 large eggs

1 teaspoon (5 ml) pure vanilla extract

Cookies are great, but they're even better when you've got a friend to share them with. In the case of luchador Mr. Iguana, that friend is his iguana sidekick.

Don't worry: We're not actually advocating a cookie diet for iguanas. Mr. Iguana's sidekick/personal mascot is a stuffed iguana named Yezka, so he actually gets to keep those sweet, buttery vanilla cookies all to himself!

If you feel like sharing, you don't need a stuffed iguana: your family and friends will do.

1. In a large bowl, sift together the flour and baking powder. Set aside.

2. In a stand mixer, cream together the butter and sugar until fluffy, 2 to 3 minutes. Add the eggs, one at a time, mixing after each addition. Scrape the sides of the bowl with a rubber spatula to ensure that all the egg is incorporated. Stir in the vanilla.

3. Add the flour mixture little by little, mixing on low speed until all the flour is incorporated. It will come together and form a smooth, pliable dough.

4. Roll the dough into a ball, then flatten into a disk. Cover with plastic wrap and refrigerate for 1 hour, or as long as overnight.

5. Position a rack in the middle position of the oven. Preheat the oven to 400°F (200°C). Line a baking sheet with parchment paper or a silicone liner.

6. On a lightly floured work surface, use a rolling pin to roll out the dough to ½ inch (1.3 cm) thick.

7. Use cookie cutters that are about 3 inches (7.5 cm) across to cut out cookies, then transfer to the prepared baking sheet.

8. Bake for about 20 minutes, or until the edges are golden. Remove from the oven and let cool for several minutes before transferring to a wire rack to cool completely.

LADY MARAVILLA

 FROM   **MONTERREY, NUEVO LEÓN, MEXICO**   ◆   **DEBUT**   **FEBRUARY 2009**

SHARING MUCH IN common with her longtime friend and oftentimes rival Keyra, Lady Maravilla also began training for her career at a very young age. But while Maravilla and Keyra share a love for dishing out dropkicks and breaking hearts, the midtwenties Maravilla has also proven to be a very capable high flyer. These two sides to the Maravilla coin also play out in her personality. One moment, she can be the bubbly "masked girl next door," and the next, she's a treacherous ruda—breaking hearts and rules.

She has had a number of classic matches around the turn of the decade including a rare women's apuestas Hair vs. Hair match against Big Mami at Lucha Libre AAA's Guerra de Titanes annual event. Despite the loss in the singles match, Lady Maravilla still maintains some pride and status in AAA as she and third-generation wrestler Villano III Jr. won the Lucha Libre AAA Mixed Tag-Team Championship, a title unique to lucha libre where one man and one woman form a "mixed" team.

FUN FACTS

★ Lady Maravilla was a mainstay on the independent lucha libre scene in Mexico before also starting to wrestle for CMLL in 2017 and then heading to Lucha Libre AAA in 2018.

★ US fans are getting to know her well from her matches on IMPACT Wrestling as well as from Lucha Libre AAA events now that they stream live for free on Twitch and are archived on YouTube.

★ When she lost the Hair vs. Hair match to Big Mami, she followed through on her bet and had her head shaved completely bald. Ever since then, she has worn a knit cap in her matches while her hair grows back.

NEAPOLITAN FLAN

SERVES
8

5 tablespoons (55 g) sugar

1 cup (240 ml) evaporated milk

1 cup (240 ml) sweetened condensed milk

6 large eggs

2 tablespoons (30 ml) pure vanilla extract

2 cream-filled wafer cookies (e.g., Pepperidge Farms Pirouettes), each cut into 4 pieces, for topping

Although Lady Maravilla is one of the baddest ruda luchadoras in the sport today, at least her desserts have a sweet side to them. There's a lot to love about flan: It's creamy, it's rich, and it's got plenty of caramel. Even the staunchest luchador in training can't resist its sweet siren call.

This decadent version is made using a mix of sweetened condensed milk and evaporated milk, which both have excess water removed and help it attain an unbelievably creamy and smooth texture. Baked in a pan and served like slices of pie with pretty cookies on top, this tricked-out version of the classic is absolutely flan-tastic.

1. Position a rack in the middle position of the oven. Preheat the oven to 350°F (180°C).

2. Make the caramel: In a pot, combine 1 tablespoon (15 ml) of water and the sugar. Heat over medium heat until the sugar begins to liquefy into caramel. Pour into a 9-inch (23 cm) round pan to harden.

3. In a medium-size bowl, stir all the remaining ingredients together except the cookies. Add to pan with caramel.

4. Create a water bath: Fill a pan slightly larger than the one you poured the ingredients into halfway with water. Carefully place the smaller pan inside the larger one so that the smaller one is nestled in the larger, water-filled pan. Be very careful to avoid letting water slosh into the smaller pan.

5. Cover the entire two-pan unit with foil and gently place it in the oven. Bake for about 45 minutes, or until a knife inserted in the center comes out clean. If you'd like the top to be browned, remove the foil and bake for an additional 10 minutes.

6. Remove from the oven and let cool briefly before transferring to the refrigerator. Refrigerate for several hours to set.

7. To serve, cut into eight slices and top each slice with a portion of cookie.

AREZ

 MEXICO CITY, MEXICO ✦ **MAY 2007**

I N A WRESTLING world filled with guys practicing *strong style* (very hard punches and kicks, very realistic style) and *even sneaky style* (the art of cheating), it was only a matter of time before someone adopted *strange style*. That luchador turned out to be Arez, a talent who makes an impression the moment you see him pop out from behind the curtain, painted from head to toe like a comic book villain. But while the look may grab you, the total package of high flying, mat wrestling, and endless creativity is what keeps you around as Arez works his magic. There are many innovators in lucha libre today, but when it comes to the king of strange style, Arez is in a class by himself.

FUN FACTS

★ Arez is one of the few luchadores in history to voluntarily unmask themselves, as opposed to losing their mask in an apuestas match (Mask vs. Mask, Hair vs. Hair, and Mask vs. Hair being the most common).

★ He came to fame as part of the stable Los Indystrongtibles, a trio of independent luchadores consisting of Arez, Belial, and Impulso (see page 146).

★ Trainers include such legends as Blue Demon Jr., Gran Apache, and Skayde.

PAY DE LIMŌN (NO-BAKE LEMON PIE)

SERVES
4 to 8

Juice of 5 large lemons (about 15 tablespoons)

1 (11.5-ounce [339 ml]) can evaporated milk

1 (13.6-ounce [387 g]) can sweetened condensed milk

2 (7-ounce [198 g]) tubes María cookies (e.g., Goya brand; about 70 cookies total)

Nope—ice cream isn't the only hot-weather dessert option. When it's hot and you can't be bothered to turn on the oven, this easy recipe for *pay de limón* is just the ticket.

Independent luchador Arez may not come from a luchador lineage, but he grew up watching the sport with fascination. Those were the same years that his mother would make this layered lemon dessert for his birthdays, so the memories are linked.

This dessert is ridiculously easy to prepare and is appropriate even for people who say they have no cooking or baking ability. It's a popular party favorite in Mexico, and it's bound to become a new favorite in your home.

1. In a blender or by hand in a large bowl, combine the lemon juice, evaporated milk, and sweetened condensed milk. Blend until all the ingredients are well mixed.

2. Arrange a layer of cookies to cover the bottom of a large, flat-based glass bowl. Then, spoon enough of the lemon mixture to cover the cookies. Repeat, alternating layers of cookies and filling, until you've exhausted your supplies.

3. Refrigerate for 3 to 4 hours to let the flavors come together.

SEGAN FRIEND

(aka Misterfriend)

 LONDON, BY WAY OF KENYA

LUCHA VAVOOM (see page 88) may be owned by Liz Fairbairn and Rita D'Albert, but there has not been a VaVOOM show since 2006 in which Segan Friend was not intimately involved. He may be British, but he's the Swiss Army knife of the VaVOOM enterprise. Using his background as an artist, Friend designs all the imagery, masks, merchandise, marketing, and media pieces for the group. His event posters often feel inspired by classic lucha libre film posters and lobby cards and add one more element to making Lucha VaVOOM stand out from everything else in lucha libre. His alter ego, a DJ named Sonic Ape, can be found providing the live soundtrack to VaVOOM shows. His Misterfriend moniker is how he is known outside of Lucha VaVOOM, heading a design company by the same name.

MEXICAN MASKED WRESTLING & HIGH OCTANE PERFORMANCE

LUCHA VaVOOM

HALLOWEEN!

OCT 23RD & 24TH
2019

FIESTA
FANTASMA

THE
MAYAN
Theatre
1038 S HILL ST
DTLA
21+

ticketweb

LUCHAVAVOOM.COM @LUCH

TRADITIONAL LEMON MARMALADE

MAKES ABOUT
5
16-ounce jars

1 pound (455 g) lemons (about 5 lemons), washed, rinds on, buttons (where the stalk attaches) removed

2 pounds (905 g) sugar

Forget lemonade! When life gives you lemons, make this lemon marmalade instead. This recipe by Segan Friend of Lucha VaVOOM makes a memorable marmalade that strikes the perfect balance of sweet and sour.

Use it in any number of ways: as a topping for toast, a mix-in for yogurt, a filling for cakes, or (*shh!*) just eat it by the spoonful. Best of all, the recipe makes a big batch, so you'll have enough to share with family or friends.

1. Place a small plate in the freezer. You'll use it later to test whether the marmalade is properly set.
2. In a large saucepan or pot over high heat, combine the lemons and 5¼ cups (1.25 L) of water. Bring to a boil, then lower the heat and cover.
3. Simmer for 2½ hours, or until the lemon rinds are very soft and easy to pierce with a fork. Remove from the heat and let the liquid cool enough that you can handle the lemons.
4. Remove the lemons. Slice them in half on a shallow dish so you can reserve any liquid released; pour any excess liquid back into the pot.
5. Remove the pips (see "What are pips?") and place them in a small muslin bag.

6. With the pips removed, slice the lemons to about ¼-inch (6 mm) thick and 1 inch (2.5 cm) long, but if you don't like "bits" in your marmalade, slice more finely.

7. Measure the liquid left in the pan. You need 3 to 3¼ cups (710 to 769 ml) of liquid. If you have more than that, bring the mixture to a boil to reduce it down; if you have less, add water to bring it to the correct level.

8. Add the chopped lemons and the muslin bag of pips.

9. Bring the mixture to a boil; add the sugar, stirring constantly to help it dissolve.

10. Boil for about 20 minutes, closely monitoring the mixture and adjusting the temperature to keep it from boiling over (that can be very messy!).

11. To test doneness, drop some of the mixture on top of the plate you put in the freezer and let it sit for a minute. It should wrinkle easily when pushed with your finger. If not, keep boiling the mixture for 2 to 3 minutes and try again.

12. Remove from the heat and let the mixture sit for 15 minutes. Remove the bag of pips; stir the mixture in one direction to reduce the bubbles that may have formed on the surface. Transfer to five clean 16-ounce (473 ml) jars and seal immediately.

What are pips?

In the world of fruit, these are the small, hard seeds in such fruits as oranges, lemons, apples, or pears.

Note:

The jars need to be sterilized in boiling hot water for 10 minutes and the marmalade should be kept in the fridge afterward.

VERONICA YUNE

 LOS ANGELES, CA

A FORMER BURLESQUE performer, Veronica Yune joined Lucha VaVOOM initially as a ring girl, spending five years escorting luchadores to the ring during shows. That all changed after Yune read up about aerial hoop performances and decided to try it. At first using aerial tissue (also known as aerial silks), Yune was approached by Lucha VaVOOM about trying a Lyra Aerial Hoop/Aerial Ring act for the shows. Four years later, Yune's act has become one of the staples of the Lucha VaVOOM experience, her aerial hoop act thrilling audiences show after show.

FUN FACTS

* Between her appearances as a valet and an aerial hoop performer, Yune has been in the wrestling business for seven years.

* She's married to luchador Zokre (see page 240), one half of the Los Luchas tag team with luchador Phoenix Star, a very well-respected SoCal-based tag team who are part of the Lucha VaVOOM world as well, but under different secret personas.

VEGAN HORCHATA CUPCAKES

MAKES
12
cupcakes

1¼ cups (155 g) all-purpose flour

1 teaspoon (2.3 g) ground cinnamon

2 tablespoons (16 g) cornstarch

½ teaspoon (2.3 g) baking soda

¾ teaspoon (3.5 g) baking powder

¼ teaspoon (1.5 g) kosher salt

1 cup (240 ml) unsweetened rice milk

1 teaspoon (5 ml) cider vinegar

⅓ cup (80 ml) canola oil

¾ cup (150 g) granulated sugar

1 teaspoon (5 ml) pure vanilla extract

½ teaspoon (2.5 ml) almond extract

RECIPE CONTINUED >

Lucha VaVOOM performer Veronica Yune is picky about sweets, so when a dessert gets her seal of approval, you know it's gonna be good. When her cousin Amy introduced her to these magical morsels at a gathering, she fell in love: vegan horchata cupcakes! What's not to love?

You'll never miss the dairy in these delectable treats, which feature sweet, spicy cake and an irresistible horchata-flavored frosting.

NOTE: Since vegan cupcakes don't have eggs to keep them fluffy and light, it's important to avoid overmixing; otherwise the cakes can become heavy and dense.

1. Position a rack in the middle position of the oven. Preheat the oven to 350°F (180°C). Line a cupcake tin with twelve paper liners.

2. In a large bowl, sift together the flour, cinnamon, cornstarch, baking soda, baking powder, and salt.

3. In a medium-size bowl, whisk together the rice milk, vinegar, canola oil, granulated sugar, and vanilla and almond extracts. Mix well.

4. Mix the dry ingredients into the wet until well combined; do not overmix.

FROSTING:

½ cup (100 g) vegan butter, at room temperature

½ cup (100 g) vegetable shortening

3½ cups (420 g) confectioners' sugar, sifted

½ teaspoon (2.3 g) ground cinnamon

1 teaspoon (5 ml) pure vanilla extract

¼ teaspoon (1.3 ml) almond extract

¼ cup (60 ml) unsweetened rice milk (you may not use all of it)

5. Divide the batter evenly among the twelve cupcake liners.

6. Bake for 20 minutes, or until a toothpick inserted into the center of a cupcake comes out clean. Remove from the oven and let cool.

7. While the cupcakes cool, make the frosting: In a medium-size bowl or in the bowl of a stand mixer, cream together the vegan butter and shortening for 3 to 5 minutes, or until fluffy.

8. Add the confectioners' sugar, cinnamon, and vanilla and almond extracts. Beat to combine; the mixture will be thick.

9. Add the rice milk, 1 tablespoon (15 ml) at a time, until the mixture has reached your desired spreading consistency.

10. Apply the frosting to the cooled cupcakes, using a spatula or piping bag.

featuring

DRINKS & BEVERAGES

★ SALUD! ★

VICTOR KHOUSTEKIAN

 SACRAMENTO, CA

COFFEE IS NOT necessarily something one would immediately associate with lucha libre; that is, unless you happen to live in Sacramento, California, where Luchador Coffee is on its way to becoming a household name. But why blend lucha libre and coffee?

Victor was first introduced to lucha libre while watching late-night Spanish TV with his grandfather when he was around six years old. His passion for lucha would reignite when the animated series *Mucha Lucha!* debuted on TV. As Victor grew older, he began to study the history of the sport. It was also around this time that he would often visit the house of a friend whose family had an affinity for the classic El Santo movies. This world of superheroes in films that you could see actually wrestle in real life greatly intrigued the now teenager and only fueled his love of the sport even further. Still a huge fan today, he lists Rey Mysterio and Penta Zero M (see page 94) as his favorite luchadores.

Outside lucha libre, Victor is most passionate about food and drink. Growing up in the restaurant industry in both the back and front of a restaurant, his personal philosophy has always been that food, and sharing a meal with someone, is something very special. In his eyes, foods tell stories and demonstrate traditions of the past. While growing up, his favorite drink was Mexican hot chocolate, especially when it was made with authentic Ibarra or Abuelita chocolate. Horchata, and the drink's sweet, creamy, cinnamony flavor, was a close second. Victor's own *abuelita* would make both drinks for him.

Although his family had been in the restaurant business, Victor knew he wanted to head in a different direction. Reasoning that the best conversations he has had and many of the best relationships he has created were all started over coffee, he decided he'd try to make it on his own. Victor knew that he was going to need something to make his coffee shop stand out, which is when he drew upon his passion for lucha libre. At only twenty-five years old, Victor opened his shop and Luchador Coffee was born.

Many of the different drinks Victor serves are inspired by his childhood and the deep roots of Mexican cuisine and tradition. Incorporating chocolate and cinnamon into a variety of drinks is one expression of that. When it comes to foods, there are many ways to find (or cook) such dishes as Victor's favorite, cochinita pibil (see Juventud Guerrera's recipe for it on page 114), but the only place you will find these special lucha libre–related drinks is at Luchador Coffee.

CHAMPUR-RUDO

SERVES
6 to 8

- 2 ounces (55 g) Luchador Coffee Abismo Negro Dark Roast coffee (or your preferred dark roast coffee) beans, coarsely ground
- ½ cup (115 g) packed dark brown sugar
- 2 (3.3-ounce [93 g]) Ibarra or Abuelita chocolate tablets
- 2 cinnamon sticks
- 1 cup (112 g) masa harina (corn flour)

Chocolate lovers will think they've died and gone to heaven when they try this version of the classic Mexican chocolate drink called *champurrado*, which is kind of like atole's superchocolaty cousin.

This version, from Victor Khoustekian of Luchador Coffee, is supercharged and extra zippy thanks to the addition of plenty of dark coffee and brown sugar. He calls it Champu-rudo, a play on words, because in the lucha world, *rudo* means "bad guy."

Coffee-wise, Khoustekian knows his stuff: From a very young age, his mother would take him to different coffee spots in town and he always dreamed of having a shop of his own. This recipe marries his passion for coffee and Mexican traditions. It's luchador approved and guaranteed to get your motor running.

1. Place the ground coffee in a fine-mesh cheesecloth. Gather into a pouch and tie the top with a kitchen string.
2. In a large saucepan or lead-free Mexican clay pot, combine 8 cups (1.9 L) of water and the coffee pouch.
3. Heat until boiling. Add the brown sugar, then lower the heat and simmer for 4 to 5 minutes, or until the sugar has dissolved.
4. Add the two chocolate tablets to the still-simmering mixture. Stir continuously, 8 to 10 minutes, until completely dissolved. Remove from the heat. Add the cinnamon sticks and let them sit in the mixture to infuse it with flavor.

5. Meanwhile, in a separate bowl, whisk together 2 cups (475 ml) of water and the masa harina until it forms a creamy, clump-free mixture. Set aside.

6. Remove the coffee pouch from the chocolate mixture. Add the masa mixture to the chocolate mixture and whisk vigorously over medium heat to bring the mixture to a boil.

7. Once the mixture reaches a boil, lower the heat to a simmer. Stir constantly over low heat for 15 minutes, or until the mixture thickens.

8. Serve in your favorite mugs.

HORCHATA ON THE ROCKS

SERVES
2 or 3

6 ounces brewed Luchador Coffee Abismo Negro Dark Roast coffee (or your preferred dark roast)

2 cups (380 g) uncooked white rice

2 cinnamon sticks

1 cup (145 g) whole almonds with skin

½ cup (100 g) sugar

½ teaspoon pure vanilla extract

2 teaspoons (scant 5 g) ground cinnamon, for sprinkling

It's hard to improve a classic like horchata, a traditional Mexican beverage made from sweetened and spiced rice and almond milk—hard, but not impossible. Victor Khoustekian of Luchador Coffee in Sacramento (which just so happens to be a known luchador hangout) offers up a delicious version of the classic beverage, then makes it a totally new experience with the addition of homemade coffee ice cubes. As the cubes melt, they infuse the horchata with a rich coffee flavor—a perfectly refreshing and energizing treat.

1. Pour hot coffee in a silicone ice cube mold. It will make four to eight cubes, depending on your tray. Chill until frozen.

2. In a large bowl or pitcher, combine 6 cups (1.4 L) of water, rice, cinnamon sticks, and almonds. Cover, and let soak for 8 to 12 hours in the refrigerator.

3. Transfer the liquid mixture to a blender and blend for 2 to 3 minutes, or until mostly smooth (there will be some texture to the mixture because of the rice).

4. Pour the mixture through fine cheesecloth or a metal strainer twice to strain into a large pitcher; press the mixture to encourage as much liquid as possible into the pitcher.

5. Stir in the sugar and vanilla.

6. Remove the coffee ice cubes from the freezer and divide evenly between two or three cups.

7. Pour the horchata over the coffee ice cubes; sprinkle the ground cinnamon on top. Enjoy immediately!

TORITO NEGRO

 NEZAHUALCÓYOTL, MEXICO ◆ **JANUARY 2017**

THE CRASH PROMOTION out of Tijuana has become a showcase promotion for young luchadores that really know how to fly. Torito Negro is one of the most notable, bursting into the promotion in 2017 as The Crash was beginning to get hot. Since then, he has wowed fans with spectacular athleticism and big-time matches against Tiago and X-Peria in The Crash's junior division. With more and more matches piling up around Mexico City, including for IWRG and its TV show, it is only a matter of time before this live wire in his early twenties gets a shot at the big time.

FUN FACTS

* Torito Negro is the son of Toro Negro Jr., grandson of Toro Negro, and nephew of Ring of Honor star and famous luchador Flamita.

* He was trained by his father (Toro Negro Jr.) and his uncle (Flamita).

* He won The Crash Junior Championship in May 2018 and held it for six months before losing it to X-Peria.

MICHELADA

MAKES
1
serving

About 2 tablespoons (30 ml)
   Chamoy sauce

About 4 teaspoons (20 g) salt or
   Tajín Clásico seasoning

Valentina sauce

Maggi Jugo seasoning sauce

Juice of 1 lime (about 3 tablespoons [45 ml])

1 (12-ounce [355 ml]) bottle of
   Mexican lager beer

As a luchador, Torito Negro is undoubtedly hot: He's constantly wowing his fans with his impressive athleticism and mounting list of big-name matches.

So, how does he cool that inner fire when the day's work is done? With a Michelada, of course! In case you're not familiar, the Michelada is a masterpiece of Mexican mixology: beer infused with chile and lime and served in a salt-rimmed glass. If you love beer, this refreshing yet fiery beverage is bound to become your new favorite way to imbibe. Check out the recipe notes below for more information on the ingredients featured in this recipe.

1. Pour the Chamoy sauce into a small, shallow dish.

2. Turn a pint-size (475 ml) glass upside down on top of the Chamoy sauce to cover the rim of the glass with sauce.

3. Pour the salt into a separate small, shallow dish. Dip the Chamoy-coated rim of the glass in the granules so the rim of the glass is evenly coated.

4. Turn the glass right side up and add a few splashes each of Valentina sauce, Maggi sauce, and lime juice. Using a spoon, mix to combine.

5. Add ice and pour your favorite Mexican lager beer on top. Enjoy immediately!

COOL YOUR INNER
fine when the day is done!

STEP THREE COAT THE RIM WITH SALT.

Not familiar with some of the recipe ingredients?

Here's a cheat sheet:

Chamoy: This is a Mexican condiment made from fruit jam, chiles, and lime juice. Its sticky texture makes it perfect for helping salt stick to the rim of the glass in this recipe; if you're unable to find it, a lime rubbed along the rim of the glass will do.

Tajin: This is a Mexican seasoning. There are several varieties, but usually they feature chile peppers, lime, and salt. It's one of those "tastes good on everything" types of toppings.

Valentina sauce: This is a Mexican hot sauce; if you're unable to find it, any pourable hot sauce, such as Tapatío, will work.

Maggi Jugo seasoning sauce: This is a Mexican sauce made from vegetable proteins. Although it's similar to soy sauce, it doesn't actually contain soy. Soy sauce can be substituted in this recipe.

SKINNY TEQUILA SUNRISE

MAKES
2
drinks

- 2 (1.5-ounce [44 ml]) shots 100% agave tequila
- 2 (0.14-ounce [3.96 g]) single-serve packets of Crystal Light lemonade or citrus drink mix
- 1 (16-ounce [475 ml]) bottle water
- 2 tablespoons (30 ml) Jordan's Skinny Syrup Strawberry or Mango zero-calorie sugar-free syrup (optional)
- Fresh lime juice (optional)

Living *la vida* sugar-free? Don't worry, you can still have a fancy cocktail! This recipe is the perfect combination of the two sides of Sylvia Muñoz. On the one hand, she's the responsible co-owner of SBWA. On the other hand, she's also evil Luchafer luchadora Alacrana Plata.

This recipe strikes the perfect balance of light and virtuous but with a mischievous kick. It's perfect for luchadores (and, you know, regular people) who want to keep sugar consumption in check—but it's still got the intoxicating effects of agave tequila. *Salud!*

1. Pour a shot of tequila each into two tall highball glasses (heck, even a red Solo cup will do) with ice.
2. Pour the contents of the Crystal Light packets into the bottle of water. Replace the cap and shake to mix.
3. Divide between the two glasses and add sugar-free syrup and/or lime juice to taste.

See pages 32–34 for Sylvia Muñoz's story and Spanish Rice recipe and page 86 for her Chicken Chorizo Chimichangas recipe.

TIGER CASAS

 MEXICO CITY, MEXICO • **FEBRUARY 2006**

ONE OF MEXICO'S well-known lucha libre families is the Casas family. As a third-generation luchador, Tiger and brother Puma King have an extensive family who are not only involved in lucha libre, but many are considered among the greatest luchadores of all time.

José "Pepe" Casas Granados began his lucha career during the early 1960s as a wrestler, then as a referee, and then became a successful trainer for both CMLL and AAA promotions. It was as a referee where Pepe gained a large part of his fame, as he would be seen every week wearing his trademark headband as he called the action for two of the largest lucha libre companies in the world. He was also famous as the father of three highly regarded luchadores: Negro Casas, El Felino, and Heavy Metal.

Negro Casas, as the oldest son, started in lucha libre first and has gone on to become one of the greatest in-ring performers in the history of the

sport. Pepe's second oldest son, El Felino, has been one of CMLL's top stars for many years. His third son, Heavy Metal, gained a lot of fame early in his career and appeared to be on track to be among the all-time greats but rarely performs today.

Jorge Luis Casas Ruiz debuted in 1982 after training with his father, Pepe, and Raul Reyes. When he first started in lucha, Jorge was called Babe Casas in press and was considered, with older brother Negro Casas, to be among the best up-and-coming luchadores in Mexico. Later, while working for CMLL, Jorge took to wearing a full body suit and mask that resembled a cat and wrestled under the name El Felino. Jorge wore the mask and covered his identity until losing his mask in an apuestas match when La Sombra took his mask on March 19, 2010, at Arena México. During the 1980s, his quick-footed style in the ring earned him the nickname "the fastest luchador."

While competing under the mask, El Felino had

two sons that entered the world of lucha libre. His oldest son took on the name Tiger Kid, while his other son took the name Puma Kid. Both names and costumes were inspired by their father. Each wore masks that also resembled cats in honor of the mask their father wore.

Early in their careers, Puma Kid and Tiger Kid originally claimed that El Felino was their uncle and not their father. After losing his mask and proclaiming his identity as Jorge Casas, he confirmed publicly that Tiger Kid and Puma Kid were indeed his children. As is customary in lucha libre, a masked wrestler's real name is kept a private and confidential fact. Tiger Kid, the son of El Felino, is often referred to as Tiger, Tiger Kid, or Tiger Casas, since it is well known that he is part of the Casas dynasty, yet his real name has not been released publicly.

Tiger Casas started training at a very young age with his father and uncles and then continued with CMLL trainers Franco Columbo, El Satánico, Ringo Mendoza, El Hijo del Gladiador, and Virus. While training, Tiger Casas started competing in Mexico's independent scene, including wrestling for the promotion owned by another large lucha family, the Moreno's IWRG promotion based out of Naucalpan.

During this time, he worked for some of the CMLL smaller arenas in cities across Mexico to gain much needed experience. After some seasoning, he moved on to wrestling in opening matches

at both Arena Coliseo and Arena México, often competing against his brother Puma or as a tag team with him. For many years he and his brother would work low on the cards at major shows while continuing to gain experience wrestling around Mexico. CMLL is known for having young talent move slowly through its ranks. In 2018, his brother Puma, in something of a shock, left CMLL to work for AAA and compete on the independent scene internationally.

Tiger decided to remain loyal to CMLL as he continued to prove his value to the oldest wrestling promotion in the world. Now, as a fifteen-year veteran of lucha libre, Tiger has worked his way up the cards in CMLL and will often be seen in main events teaming with his father or his uncle Negro Casas.

The year 2020 started off with his international expansion when he made his debut with New Japan Pro-Wrestling, competing in its annual Fantastica Mania tour that lasted eight nights.

For the Casas family, lucha libre is not only an affair for the male members. El Felino's second wife, Princesa Blanca, stepmother to Tiger and Puma, had a career in lucha libre that spanned more than twenty years before retiring in 2014 after losing her hair in an apuestas match at Arena México.

Their aunt, Dalys La Caribeña, is married to their uncle Negro Casas and is one of the most successful luchadoras of the last decade. She held

the CMLL Women's World Championship for over two and a half years, making her the longest champion of all the 2010s and the second longest of all time.

Through the marriage of Negro Casas and Dalys, Tiger's extended lucha family grew even larger, adding Veneno (Dalys's brother) and four cousins: Canelo Casas, Danny Casas, Destroyer, and Nanyzh Rock. Rumor has it there are even more Casas family members in the sport, but this

is unconfirmed because a masked luchador's true identity is usually not revealed until he or she loses an apuestas match.

With a family legacy spanning generations, and his father and uncle considered among the best luchadores of all time, Tiger has a lot to live up to. But it is a challenge he has not shied away from and a legacy to which he is firmly committed to upholding. So far, this cat is on the right track.

SUPERPOWERED PROTEIN SHAKE

MAKES
1
serving

1 large ripe banana

11 ounces (325 ml) whole milk

½ cup (40 g) rolled oats

About 4 large fresh strawberries, hulled

½ cup (75 g) fresh blueberries

½ cup (48 g) protein powder of your choice (optional)

Ground cinnamon, for garnish

With great power comes great responsibility. Tiger Casas is a third-generation luchador, hailing from a family that is basically considered royalty in the sport. That means there are a lot of eyes on him and his brother Puma King (yep, also a luchador), as well as very high expectations.

In his heyday, his father Felino was known as the Fastest Luchador. It takes a lot of stamina to live up to the family legend, and Tiger does it with this superpowered protein shake. The recipe, as well as the finished result, is simple yet sweet, but it's bound to fill you with some killer energy. Try it for yourself and see if it helps you channel your inner Tiger!

1. In a blender, combine all the ingredients, except the cinnamon. Blend until the mixture reaches your desired consistency. Garnish with cinnamon.

NOTES: If not using protein powder, consider adding ice to augment the texture.

Not a fan of dairy milk? Feel free to use your favorite nondairy alternative, but note that it may alter the texture of the finished shake.

HAYASHI MASAHIRO

 KOBE, JAPAN

WHEN YOU TALK to people about lucha libre, one of the first things people talk about are the colorful masks and outrageous outfits. Do you ever wonder who creates your favorite luchadores' masks?

Hayashi Masahiro is the man responsible for designing the outfits and masks of Rey Mysterio, arguably the most famous luchador worldwide. Hayashi's first exposure to Rey Mysterio came in 1995 when the luchador made his initial trip to Japan for the now famous Super J Cup Second Stage tournament. That year, he was not part of the tournament itself but was brought in with Psicosis as a featured attraction match.

Prior to witnessing Rey Mysterio battle Psicosis, Hayashi had a career in creating masks and costumes. Like many kids in Japan his age, he grew up watching and becoming a fan of the original Tiger Mask. As time passed, his interest in lucha libre

grew and his desire to collect masks of luchadores began. By the time he was twenty years old, he had amassed quite a collection of masks.

This hobby morphed into a career in designing and producing outfits and masks for luchadores. Seeing Rey Mysterio inspired him, which led to Hayashi designing an outfit made from a special fabric and presenting it to Rey on his next visit to Japan the following year. Since that moment, now more than two decades ago, the duo has collaborated on outfits that Rey has worn for his major matches, including his Wrestlemania and Triplemanía bouts.

Hayashi also operates the website Solucha .com, which carries unique merchandise, such as ring-worn vintage masks, toys, autographs, and more. Hayashi also published a book called *The Art and Magic of the Mask*, which is a guide for fans to understand the history and importance of vintage mask makers.

TEPACHE

SERVES
8

- 4 ounces (113 g) piloncillo, broken into pieces, plus more to taste
- 1 cinnamon stick
- 2 whole cloves
- ½ medium-size pineapple, including skin and core, cut into chunks
- Sugar, to taste

Hayashi may be best known as Japan's most famous mask maker for star luchadores, such as Rey Mysterio (for whom he has made masks now for over twenty years, including his time in WCW and WWE), but he's also got a sweet tooth.

He's taken fifty-plus trips to Mexico in the past twenty years, but it wasn't until after more than ten years of traveling there that he tried tepache, a sweetened beverage that he describes as "kind of like Mexican root beer." A friend recommended that he try it with *cemitas* (a type of torta) and he's been hooked ever since.

Although he's never quite been able to replicate the original at home, this recipe comes pretty close. It features *piloncillo*, a type of unrefined dark brown sugar, along with cinnamon, cloves, and pineapple.

NOTE: Can't find piloncillo at your grocery store? Dark brown sugar can be substituted.

1. In a large pot, bring 8 cups (1.9 L) of water to a boil.
2. Remove from the heat and add the piloncillo. Stir to help the sugar dissolve.
3. Once the piloncillo has dissolved, add the cinnamon stick, cloves, and pineapple chunks.
4. Cover the pot with a dish towel or other breathable material that will protect the tepache while it ferments.

5. Let the mixture sit at room temperature for at least 24 hours to ferment. The longer it sits, the more complex the flavor will become. You'll see white foam on the mixture; this is a sign that the fermentation is at work.

6. Once you've attained your desired level of fermentation, strain the mixture into a pitcher to remove any solid matter. Add sugar to taste; store in the refrigerator.

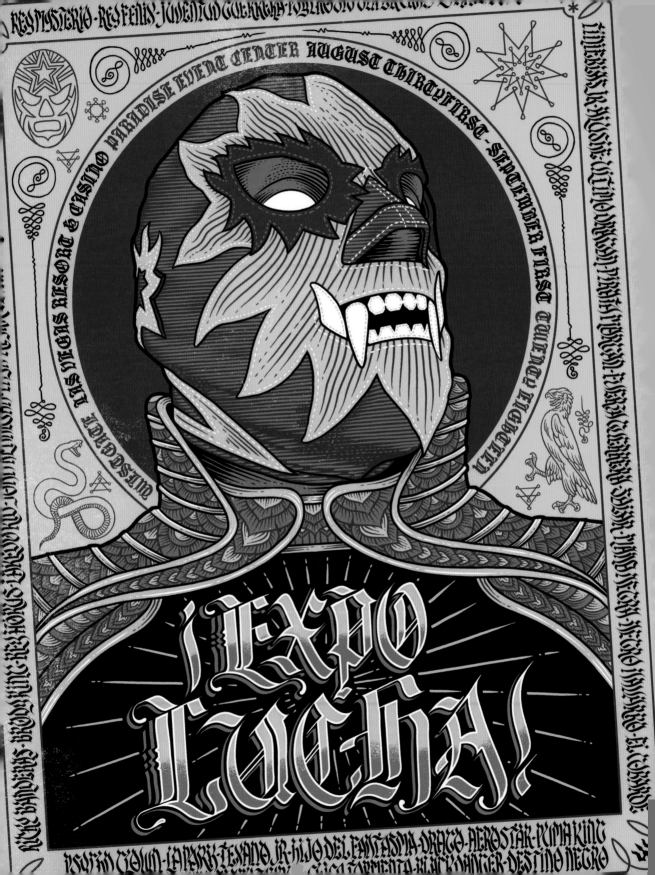

ACKNOWLEDGMENTS

THIS BOOK IS the result of the contributions of so many luchadores and others associated with our great sport, so first I want to thank each and every contributor as well as their families who have passed down so many of the amazing recipes in the book.

I would like to thank Masked Republic and Legends of Lucha Libre's Ruben Zamora and Kevin Kleinrock for having faith in me to bring my family history and the stories of so many other lucha libre families to light in the pages of this book. It has been an honor to be able to share not only the personal stories but the favorite foods that bond our families together—or that sometimes are simply just our favorites.

The biographies and stories you have read throughout could not have been completed without the help of my LuchaCentral.com teammates Eric Mutter, Matt Farmer, Pep Carrera, and Rick Mandell.

While each recipe came to me firsthand by the book's wonderful contributors, preparing them for you to be able to easily follow and re-create in your own homes has been made possible by the efforts of Jessie Moore, Alejandra Medina Cavallo, Berenice Montoya Romero, Ittoh Rodríguez, and Irmia Aven.

No book related to lucha libre could ever be truly complete without photography to give readers a look into our amazing, colorful, and dynamic world. So, thank you to our incredible contributing photographers Jerry Villagrana, Josh "Rudos Photo" Garcia, Jose "El Pollo" Gil, Oscar "King Studio" Rodriguez, George Tahinos, Daniela Herrerías, Kevin Quiroz, Katie Grays, Black Terry Jr., and Andrés Aquino.

Finally, thank you, dear reader, for your own desire to learn more about the great history and culture of lucha libre and wanting to EAT LIKE A LUCHADOR!

INDEX

Index

Index

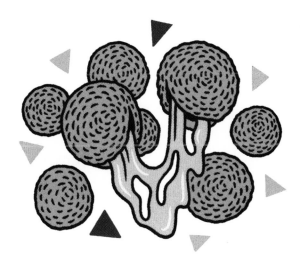